I0045967

The ART of Responsible Communication

The ART of Responsible Communication

Leading with Values Every Day

David L. Remund, PhD

BEP BUSINESS EXPERT PRESS

The ART of Responsible Communication
Copyright © Business Expert Press, LLC, 2015.

All rights reserved. No part of this publication may be reproduced, stored in a retrieval system, or transmitted in any form or by any means—electronic, mechanical, photocopy, recording, or any other except for brief quotations, not to exceed 400 words, without the prior permission of the publisher.

First published in 2015 by
Business Expert Press, LLC
222 East 46th Street, New York, NY 10017
www.businessexpertpress.com

ISBN-13: 978-1-60649-754-8 (paperback)
ISBN-13: 978-1-60649-755-5 (e-book)

Business Expert Press Giving Voice to Values on Business Ethics and Corporate Social Responsibility Collection

Collection ISSN: 2163-9477 (print)
Collection ISSN: 2163-937X (electronic)

Cover and interior design by S4Carlisle Publishing Services Private Ltd., Chennai, India

First edition: 2015

10 9 8 7 6 5 4 3 2 1

Printed in the United States of America.

Dedication

For the truly responsible leaders—
and those who desire to be.

Contents

Introduction ix

Part 1   Embracing the ART of Values-driven Leadership 1
Chapter 1 Accessibility 3
Chapter 2 Responsiveness 13
Chapter 3 Transparency 25

Part 2   Communicating Responsibly
           with Key Stakeholders 35
Chapter 4 Managers and Supervisors 37
Chapter 5 Employees and Contractors 45
Chapter 6 Investors and Regulators 57
Chapter 7 Reporters and Editors 63
Chapter 8 Customers and Prospects 71

Part 3   Leading with Values Daily—
           The ART Action Plan 81

Acknowledgments 89
Bibliography 91
About the Author 99
Index 101

Introduction

Ever feel overwhelmed by the number of people clamoring for your attention, and the many ways they do so in this digital age? You are not alone. Research suggests that most executives now spend at least half their time communicating (Silverman 2012). That communication may take the form of face-to-face meetings, conference calls, phone calls, e-mail messages, and other means. Meetings generally account for up to two full days of an executive's work week, while managing electronic communications may account for up to one full day (Krauss 2014). We are drowning in communication, or so it seems. What's a leader like you to do?

To be certain, technology, globalization, and economic pressures place incredible demands on executives and other business leaders these days. People at all levels of an organization need information, often urgently, and, above all, they need expert insight and perspective to make well-grounded decisions. As a leader, are you fully owning up to that responsibility? Are you living your values each day, and communicating as efficiently and responsibly as possible with all of your key stakeholders, both inside and outside your organization? That is, are you communicating in a way that is candid, clear, and consistent, and fully rooted in values-driven decisions, regardless of how busy you are, and how many people need your time?

If you said no, you are not alone. Communication is often a significant challenge for leaders. The good news is that you now have some helpful answers right at your fingertips. Welcome to *The ART of Responsible Communication*.

About This Book

This book is a how-to communications guide for business executives and other leaders like you. The intent is to help you identify and understand some simple yet pivotal ways in which you can take greater responsibility for communication, and substantially improve the vitality and adaptability of your colleagues and your organization. You will learn to define and honor strong values *and* better streamline your thoughts and actions, in accordance with those values. Above all, you will learn how to consistently and efficiently communicate with all those who have a vested stake in your organization. You will become an expert at responsible communication, and, in turn, relationship-building.

The primary chapters examine several key leadership principles—namely Accessibility, Responsiveness and, Transparency (thus, the acronym ART, from the book's title)—and provide you with opportunities for self-reflection, as well as actionable ideas to implement immediately. These chapters are designed for quick reading, emphasizing *why* you should be more purposefully involved in communication, and *how* you can do so without adding to your already full plate. The final chapter—comprising Part 3—organizes all of the key lessons from the book into an easy-to-skim action guide. Read the full book now for depth and full context; use Part 3 as a handy go-to resource in the months and years ahead.

Why This Book?

This book came to be because, after two decades of working with executives and other leaders, I know many like you strongly and sincerely want to do better, communication-wise. Most who lead businesses and other organizations long to see both their enterprises and employees succeed. They want to keep people informed and engaged. They want to build a strong groundswell of support. But, the world is an increasingly tough place to do business, and even more so a tough place to communicate in a truly effective fashion. We are all so damn busy and pressed for time. Even the best intentions don't always result in the most productive words or actions. To my knowledge, there hadn't been an action-oriented communication guide specifically addressing communication as a leadership responsibility, so I made it a point to write one.

By way of background, I came in and out of the mortgage industry during two separate booms, each prior to the financial collapse of 2008. There was so much money flying around in that industry during those times; normalcy was anything but the norm. I worked with teams of executives in back-to-back, all-day meetings that often stretched from sunrise to well past sunset. That's how work was nearly every weekday, regularly supplemented by weekend conference calls, business travel, and/or grinding through hundreds of backlogged e-mail messages and action items. On at least one occasion that comes to memory, I worked nearly 42 hours straight with little more than a few catnaps here and there. Balancing work demands and personal life was tough enough, let alone trying to champion personal values through solid communication. You have no doubt felt this same way, at least at times. Our desire to do good can easily get beat down by day-to-day pressures.

Let me share a story that became a touch point for me, and may be a wake-up call for you. There came a time in my corporate career when a mandate was put in place by a C-level executive, prohibiting presentations at senior-level project team meetings. All that would be allowed going forward was a single-page dashboard handout listing measurable objectives and containing two or three small charts illustrating key metrics. Nirvana? Not exactly. Twenty-minute, relatively straightforward presentations quickly became multihour, nonlinear debates full of sidebar conversations, misunderstandings, and misinterpretations. People walked in and out of the meetings at will, and there was truly no focal point for dialogue. Takeaways were unclear and inconsistent among project team members, and discord was high. Communication-wise, things simply got worse.

This story is not to defend presentations, which often fail to foster open dialogue and debate. Rather, this story illustrates that when we attempt to streamline and control communication, we often create even greater problems. Communicating effectively is rarely easy, nor is it ever a one-time, one-way action. Effective communication is a dynamic, ongoing, two-way process, and that process requires—no, that process *demands*—strong leadership principles of Accessibility, Responsiveness, and Transparency (ART), underpinned by an equally strong sense of commitment and enthusiasm.

How much or little to communicate isn't necessarily what matters most, I have found. The answer lies in *how* you communicate with the intended audience, and the tone you set with people, especially those who must follow your lead, or at least who rely on your judgment and wisdom. Perpetuate a highly controlled, stifled, and ultimately suffocating communications environment, and you'll simply reap more of what you sow. Take a more conscious, open and dynamic approach to communication, though, and you'll soon find people adapting their behavior to mirror yours. This is, truly, the ART of responsible communication.

Defining "Responsibility"

There are many ways to define responsibility, so we need to be more specific. In business, we tend to associate the concept of responsibility with legal obligation—and perhaps moral and ethical obligation, too. Let's focus in on the legal aspect, though, which underlies all business activity. The American Bar Association (1969) defines professional responsibility for its members, in a broad sense, as obeying the law, avoiding conflicts of interest, and consistently putting clients' interests ahead of one's own. Applying this concept to the aspect of leadership examined in this book, we might say that a leader's responsible communication is lawful, mutually beneficial, and other-focused. Could responsible communication really be that simple? No. If it were, there would be no need for this book.

The following pages will shed light on the many considerations that fall within the domain of responsible communication. You will come to a clearer understanding of what it means to communicate responsibly, and what it means to lead with values every day. Let me be clear: this notion of responsible communication applies to all stakeholders, not just the employees and contractors within your span of control. That means you can and should also apply the principles contained in this book to your ongoing communication with fellow managers and supervisors; investors and regulators; editors and reporters; and customers and prospects, especially those who are active on social media.

You honestly *can* make a difference. In fact, as a leader, you may be the only person who can make a difference, given your position and channels of influence. This book will help you learn how.

Inspired by Giving Voice to Values

This title that you are now reading is absolutely a book about communication. But, to be honest, this is also a book about values-based leadership. The lessons contained in *The ART of Responsible Communication* are inspired by *Giving Voice to Values: How to Speak Your Mind When You Know What's Right,* by Gentile (2010), a senior research scholar at Babson College. That book integrates examples, methods, and guidelines into a playbook for how to implement values in times of ethical conflict. *Giving Voice to Values* is not about deciding what the right thing to do is, but rather about how to get the right things accomplished. In a similar way, *The ART of Responsible Communication* is designed to help you implement values through day-to-day words and actions. The difference is that this book is written specifically for leaders like you, and with a purposeful focus on communication.

Don't worry if you have not read *Giving Voice to Values*. You will find that Gentile's guiding philosophies, relative to communication, are referenced at key points in this book. The driving intent of *The ART of Responsible Communication* is to help you, as a leader, leverage your power, time, and resources in ways that most effectively champion values. The focus is not on decision making itself, but rather on how to communicate values-based decisions as a means of sense-making and coalition-building, both within and outside of your company.

Structured to Challenge, Inspire, and Guide You

The book contains three sections: Part 1 addresses the principles of responsible leadership and communication, Part 2 examines communication strategies for each of your key stakeholder groups, and Part 3 provides a succinct action plan for putting all of these ideas into immediate motion.

Part 1 is intended to challenge your thinking about what it means to lead and to communicate, particularly in today's complex, global, technology-infused world. You will reflect on the three important leadership principles—Accessibility, Responsiveness, and Transparency—that constitute the ART of responsible communication, and learn how to put these principles into motion.

Part 2 applies the ART principles to each of your key stakeholder groups. Chapters dive into how to best communicate with other leaders and managers in your organization; employees and contractors; investors and regulators; editors and reporters; and, finally, customers and prospects, especially those who are active on social media. The purpose of Part 2 is to inspire you about the many ways in which you can put responsible communication principles into daily action.

Finally, Part 3 summarizes key takeaways from the prior two sections, in a step-by-step action plan. This brief closing section essentially serves as a clear guide for how to become a more responsible communicator and leader.

The book stays focused on your leadership role, and how that role can be more active and influential, thanks to consistent outreach with your many and diverse stakeholders. The sections and chapters allow you quick access to the areas of most interest or concern now, or as challenges shift in the future.

An Important Disclaimer

This book is not for every leader. Why? Many executives consider communication the responsibility of an internal colleague or department, not something requiring their own active involvement. These leaders tend to focus almost exclusively on financials, key performance indicators, and other metrics. That is fine—except that these numbers are nearly always lagging measures. They reveal problems only after problems have already begun to bubble to the surface.

Inevitably, employees, customers, vendors, investors, policymakers, and consumers will become disgruntled with your organization and one of its offerings or initiatives. There is just no denying; things go wrong.

You are a leader, and it is your responsibility to proactively stay in touch with key stakeholders. You can play an indispensable role in helping prevent or mediate issues, before a crisis develops and matters quickly escalate beyond organizational control via the immediacy of news media and social media.

Leaders who value efficiency and financials above all else, manage their days accordingly, and with blinders on as far as the importance of responsible communication. They see leadership as strictly science, and rarely as ART. They tend to be reactive rather than proactive when it comes to sharing information, gathering feedback, and managing issues. You? You're likely much different.

Chances are you appreciate just how powerful—and vital—candid, clear, and consistent communication is to your organization and everyone it touches, internally and externally. You are fully committed to, and actively involved in. internal and external communication, or you at least you desire to be. You wouldn't be reading this book, otherwise.

Truth be told, it isn't easy to lead an organization or operational unit *and* play an active role in multiple forms of communication. This book is designed to help. The short, pointed chapters should prove invigorating and inspiring. You will take away actionable ideas for immediate implementation, integrating the science of your technical and functional expertise with the ART of values-based leadership. These steps should result in meaningful, positive, and lasting impacts, both for the near- and long-term, as well as inside and outside of your organization.

Imagine a culture where all employees operate with values top-of-mind, and where communicating efficiently and effectively becomes the norm, rather than the exception. You can help make this kind of culture a reality for your organization.

Let's get started.

PART 1

Embracing the ART
of Values-driven Leadership

CHAPTER 1

Accessibility

One of the mid-level executives I had been mentoring for years reached out to me late one afternoon, and asked me to go for a walk together downtown. The invitation for a walk was not necessarily that unusual; more and more colleagues and peers, it seems, have discovered the simple pleasure of walking meetings, which have a unique way of invigorating body, mind, and spirit. No, the idea to go walking together wasn't the surprising part; what caught me off-guard is that this had been a Sunday afternoon, a time traditionally protected from discussions of business and professional development. What did she want so urgently want to discuss, I wondered to myself? She had begun a new role with a new, nationwide organization earlier that month, but what could have already cropped up as a pressing issue? And did this conversation *really* need to happen on a Sunday afternoon?! To be honest, I had been contemplating a short nap on the couch after a long and trying six-day week of work. Alas, I slipped on a pair of Nikes, and set out to discover the answers.

Being a leader means being accessible, simple as that. You know how important and treasured your accessibility is, I'm certain, because people clamor for your attention every day, and likely often nearly every hour of the day. Were you not accessible to anyone, you would not be a leader. And you would not be needed.

We have to prioritize, of course, though. There is only so much time in a given day, and not every request is urgent or even important. That afternoon, though, the tone of the request sent a strong signal. I simply knew being there for a valued mentee at that particular moment was far more important than a self-indulgent siesta. My accessibility mattered.

When I met up with my protégé that Sunday afternoon, we walked for several miles, in and around downtown. The topics? How to develop deeper technical expertise and establish more solid credibility within a new industry. And how to deliver bottom-line value as a newcomer—and a woman— within a conservative organization that has a mostly male leadership team. Yet what was most on my mentee's mind was how to deal with having so much access to C-suite executives and other key decision makers. What?!

Imagine if your colleagues, employees, and contractors became concerned because they had *too* much access to you. Is it even possible to imagine such a scenario? I'm guessing not. Most of us have the exact opposite problem; that is, people need or want our time, input, and guidance, and we simply cannot be there for everyone to the degree they would like.

In this situation, my mentee was just a few weeks into the new position. It's that time in the onboarding cycle when the new hire, regardless of his or her level, feels inundated with information. We sometimes call this the "drinking out of a fire hose" stage. In her case, she was not only trying to tackle a new industry, but was having to build credibility and relationships with executives, most of whom were male and significantly older than her. She had more access to these leaders than she had ever imagined, and she was drowning in opportunity. Each new meeting or conversation left her feeling more exposed and less confident. She simply needed to talk through some strategies for navigating the onslaught of data and demands, and gain some reassurance that she would live up to the promise that came with her professional reputation and earned her this opportunity in the first place. Having too much access to leaders is not a problem, I told her. Having no access, or extremely limited access, is what would really set off the alarms.

Defining Accessibility

When we think of accessibility in business, we think of making our products and services available to people of varied backgrounds and abilities. In fact, the Convention on the Rights of Persons with Disabilities generally defines accessibility as making products, devices, services, or environments available to as many people as possible (United Nations General Assembly 2006). What if this same principle applied to leaders? How would you conduct yourself, in order to make yourself as available to as many people—and as many different types of stakeholders—as possible? Would this make a significant difference, in the end? It very well could. According to research by global public relations firm, Ketchum, being seen and heard is one of the most essential elements to establishing credibility with the public, as a corporate spokesperson (Ketchum 2014). What if you applied that same approach to all key stakeholders for your organization, and be more visible and engaged, in all that you do. You would quickly realize that your leadership role provides you a unique, powerful platform, one that should not be squandered.

Imagine for a moment that you are not the leader of a business, but rather a brilliant systems analyst who just happens to be confined to home for a number of physical reasons. You are not mobile enough to leave home, even with a specially equipped vehicle, motorized wheelchair, building accommodations, and other assistive measures. Still, you are the perfect fit for a local startup's need for a software coder and project manager. What if you couldn't attend an on-site interview? Your talent would go untapped, simply because of a lack of accessibility. Or, what if you somehow made the interview, got the offer, started the position, and then realized that your body simply cannot handle the extraordinary demands of commuting to an office each day? Without some flexibility on the part of the employer, your talent would again go to waste.

Think of each of your stakeholders, and especially each of your colleagues, as a person who requires access in order to make contributions to, and investments in, your organization's long-term success. That vendor who needs a decision on a service contract? The television news reporter who seeks industry expertise for a special series airing next week? That customer who calls out your company on social media for mishandling an order? You can view situations like these as interruptions, annoyances, and distractions. Or, in the spirit of accessibility, you can view such situations as opportunities to engage with people who have a true passion for your business. Sharing a little of your time more broadly, and when appropriate, can reap rewards, both short-term and long-term.

Why Accessibility Matters

How do you treat new members of your team, or new vendors or investors? You cannot wall yourself off in your office, delegate relationship-building to a colleague, and expect a fruitful outcome. If the new hire or new interest needs direct access to you, then you must provide that access—not just in the short-term, but in a reliable and consistent manner over the long-term. Accessibility breeds trust, and trust builds relationships.

Accessibility is often about information. You are in a powerful and controlling position. Information is power, as they say; so, too, is control of situations and information. Being inaccessible means trying to control situations and prevent access to information. Being accessible means staying adaptable to changing circumstances and sharing information as freely as possible, in order to help others maximize their contributions to the organization. Your accessibility helps others feel comfortable sharing ideas and discussing situations (Quast 2013). In short, accessibility engenders trust.

Consider this possibility. You spend every Friday morning in a series of executive leadership meetings. This always puts you behind near the very end of the week. Because you value weekends and time with your family, you make it known to your staff not to interrupt you on Friday afternoons, while working in your office, unless there is an emergency. What tone are you setting? Imagine if your boss, who we will assume is the chief executive officer, told you that for one workday per week—a full 20 percent of the week, in other words—she would either be in closed-door meetings or not accessible? Is that the kind of leader you want? Is that the kind of leader you want to be for other?

Research studies across industries suggest that having access to leaders—and, therefore, having access to information—is one of the key factors that drives individual performance and organizational development (Arbab et al. 2014; Potter and Baum 2014; Waligo, Clarke, and Hawkins 2014). Do you share all that you can with your team after you have attended meetings or received executive updates? And, do you share that information in a timely fashion?

Reflect on your organization's growth or decline, and on your employees' individual contributions, or lack thereof, along the way. What role did their access to you, and their access to real-time information, play in those gains or losses? How might you have done things differently, or how might you do things differently, as you look ahead?

In her groundbreaking book, *Giving Voice to Values,* Gentile (2010) discusses further the critical importance of information to employees. The information-gathering process helps people build confidence, identify competing concerns, and, ultimately, garner allies. What if internal roadblocks impeded the gathering of information? What if your leadership style sent the signal that information is controlled at the top, and access to information is something to be granted, not pursued? Through her research and consulting, Gentile has found that the people who are able to confidently voice their values in the workplace are those who have the time and freedom to gather data and assess arguments. Do these sound like your employees, or not?

In research circles, there is a leadership model called leader-member exchange theory, or LMX, which speaks to this issue of leadership accessibility. LMX suggests that the leadership process varies across a team, based on the leader's relationship and interaction with each individual follower (Northouse 2010). In other words, not all leader-follower relationships are equal; some subordinates have close relationships with the leaders, and others have only stiff, detached relationships with the leader. Over time, in-groups and out-groups form. Relationships with the in-group demonstrate high degrees of mutual trust, respect, admiration, and influence. By contrast, relationships with the out-group are focused mostly on formal communication and based largely on job descriptions.

Think about your immediate team, and perhaps even the next level or two below your position. Are you able to recognize the in-group members? The out-group members? How does the access you provide to one group differ from the other? In what ways might you consciously address this gap? For example, you may simply make a point of investing more time with the out-group members—not necessarily developing more personal rapport, but at least demonstrating that you care about, and appreciate, the work being accomplished. When employees understand how a business operates, can connect their work to the organization's financial performance, and know what has to be done for the business to compete, they are more likely to be engaged (Herring 2008).

Of course, there are many challenges to breaking through with outgroups, and simply in making yourself more accessible to employees and other stakeholders. You may not feel you have time to listen. You may not like to hear bad news or differing opinions. You may, as already discussed, like the power that information provides you. Or, you may not simply like stakeholders who ask questions and, by default, question how you exercise authority and control. The bottom line is that companies can't innovate, respond to stakeholders, or run efficiently unless people have access to timely information (O'Toole and Bennis 2009). Be open, and be as candid as you can be. Seek and share information in more diverse ways. Encourage lively, respectful discussion and debate. Honor truth. Reward or at least recognize people who think differently and challenge the status quo.

Accessibility: Easier Said Than Done

Above all, be realistic. The simple truth is that the more successful you are, the less accessible you are (Hyatt 2012). Protect your time and energy. Prioritize your daily contacts, giving time only to those who truly need that time. Rely upon others, and delegate effectively, even when it comes to responsiveness. For every request that comes your way, think: Who should be handling this? Being the leader does not mean doing it all yourself. Rather, the productive leader is the one who realizes other people's strengths, and helps them help others and the organization move forward.

One of President Obama's dubious legacies is how he suppressed journalists' access to information, particularly interviews and investigations involving federal agencies. This trend began with the Bush administration, but escalated during the Obama years, ultimately driving the Society of Professional Journalists and 37 other watchdog groups to file a direct complain with the President himself (Hazley 2014). Most federal agencies began prohibiting direct interaction with editors and reporters, under President Obama's watch, except in instances where a public relations professional would direct or supervise the interview process. And, even in those cases, journalists would be required to provide the interview questions in advance, or only receive information if a promise were made that there would be no direct attribution within the finished news piece. President Obama made matters worse, holding only a handful of news conferences per year, and becoming the first President to routinely refuse to answer questions during brief appearances at the White House or following meetings with formal leaders (Koffler 2012).

What can you learn from President Obama's communication legacy? At the surface level, the President set the tone that information is power, and that his leadership, and his team, were not to be questioned, at least not openly and freely by news reporters and editors. Is this the type of dynamic, two-way dialogue that builds trust and respect? No. Fundamentally, is this responsible communication? Again, the answer is no.

Of course, we can't possibly know or understand all of the sensitive factors at play in running a Presidential administration. We shouldn't necessarily question leadership decisions, but we should question communication style. Trying to control information and suppress dialogue? These are rarely effective communication styles, nor are they responsible communication practices.

The world will become increasingly dynamic, demanding a more open, collaborative approach to communication and work. Business scholars Georg Vielmetter and Yvonne Sell have examined trends that will shape the way we work over the next decade or two. These include globalization, individualism, and digitization. Because of these factors and more, leadership will become increasingly uncomfortable in the future (Vielmetter and Sell 2014). You will increasingly work with technologies you don't fully understand or control. You will need to work in flattened hierarchies, where employees have more power and external stakeholders have greater influence. You will have to further blend your professional and personal lives. You will need to check your ego at the door. Your leadership role will truly be about motivating and empowering others—not trying to control them. Are you prepared for that responsibility?

This chapter and the next two focus on three essential leadership principles for responsible communication—Accessibility, Responsiveness, and Transparency. Why use the acronym ART? Because there is truly an art to responsible communication, and you should never forget that. This is an intuitive process that requires more than the science of collecting data and calculating decisions. You will need to foster dialogue and embrace debate. You will need to stay adaptable and confident. You will need to be there for the people who need you. You will need to be responsive. And you will have to get comfortable with being transparent. Yes, there is an ART to responsible communication. The sooner you get started, the sooner you will master this ART.

Reflection Questions

- **Were you not accessible to anyone, you would not be a leader. And you would not be needed.** Who needs you the most, professionally speaking? In what ways do they access you? Are you accessible as you possibly can be to them? How might you make yourself more accessible?

- **We have to prioritize. There is only so much time in a given day, and not every request is urgent or even important.** How do you know what is most important? Who most needs your attention today and in the weeks ahead? How will you make the time?

- **You can view situations as interruptions, annoyances, and distractions. Or, in the spirit of accessibility, you can view them as opportunities to engage with people who have a true passion for your business.** What situations have you recently considered annoyances? Would there have been benefit in treating such circumstances differently? How might you have made more of the moment?

- **Being inaccessible means trying to control situations and prevent access to information. Being accessible means staying adaptable to changing circumstances and sharing information as freely as possible, in order to help others maximize their contributions to the organization.** Do others generally see you as accessible or inaccessible? What specific behaviors might give them that impression of you? How could you do better?

- **Having access to leaders—and, therefore, having access to information—is one of the key factors that drives individual performance and organizational development.** How does your accessibility influence others' individual performances, as well as the overall organizational performance? In what ways might you improve your accessibility, in order to help others improve themselves?

- **Being the leader does not mean doing it all yourself.** Do you trust others? With what? How often? Could you do better at delegating? How?

Responsible Actions

- **Were you not accessible to anyone, you would not be a leader.** You have to prioritize, though. There is only so much time in a given day, and not every request is urgent or even important.
- **Think of each of your stakeholders, and especially each of your colleagues, as a person who requires access in order to make contributions to, and investments in, your organization's long-term success.** In the spirit of accessibility, view such situations as opportunities to engage with people who have a true passion for your business. Sharing a little of your time more broadly, and when appropriate, can reap rewards, both short-term and long-term.
- **You cannot wall yourself off in your office, delegate relationship-building to a colleague, and expect a fruitful outcome.** If the new hire or new interest needs direct access to you, then you must provide that access—not just in the short-term, but in a reliable and consistent manner over the long-term. Accessibility breeds trust, and trust builds relationships.
- **Being accessible means staying adaptable to changing circumstances and sharing information as freely as possible, in order to help others maximize their contributions to the organization.** Being inaccessible means trying to control situations and prevent access to information.
- **Companies can't innovate, respond to stakeholders, or run efficiently unless people have access to timely information.** Be open, and be as candid as you can be. Seek and share information in more diverse ways. Encourage lively, respectful discussion and debate. Honor truth. Reward or at least recognize people who think differently and challenge the status quo.
- **Be realistic.** Protect your time and energy. Prioritize your daily contacts, giving time only to those who truly need that time. Rely upon others, and delegate effectively, even when it comes to responsiveness. For every request that comes your way, think: Who should be handling this?

CHAPTER 2

Responsiveness

My dad managed the local office of a regional Bell System operating company, and did so through the 1984 divestiture of AT&T and beyond. Being an involved parent, a telephone industry official and a communicator at heart, he had clear expectations with me and my siblings. He expected a phone call whenever we might be late getting home from an evening out with friends. Dad believed in communication *and* responsibility.

One summer night, my high school buddies and I were out well past sundown. They had picked me up at my house earlier in the evening. After driving out in the country, the guys shared with me that they had snuck booze out of their parents' homes. I did not drink, and this was my first run-in with alcohol. I was confused, mad, and, to be honest, scared.

Had I driven myself that night, I would have just left immediately. But, I was at the mercy of these friends. Peer pressure at play, I didn't have the guts to demand a ride home, or even to the nearest pay phone to call my parents. (This was long before the days of cell phones.) I successfully avoided drinking and eventually got home safely, apologizing profusely to Dad. He didn't dress me down. Seeing that I was visibly upset, Dad listened and was empathetic. But then he simply said, "Next time, don't be sorry. Be right." With that advice, Dad was off to bed, leaving me standing alone in a darkened kitchen.

That simple lesson from long ago applies so well to leadership and responsible communication in business today. Don't be sorry for allowing situations to get out of control, or that push you and those around you toward trouble. Instead, be right. That means: do the right thing; stay laser-focused on your values, commitments, and responsibilities; remain fully engaged; monitor situations and respond immediately to issues as they develop; speak up firmly; and truly take ownership. Likewise, be there for your team, just as my dad was for me that night. Listen. Be empathetic. Offer constructive feedback and advice. Then move on, giving your team members the time and space necessary to reflect upon and integrate key lessons from important coaching moments. In short, strive to be the kind of leader and communicator that Dad was for me.

Not communicating? Not taking responsibility? Not responding to changing situations? For you, and for any other leader, those are simply not options these days. We live and work in a fast-paced economy and technology-fueled society. You can't sit meekly in the proverbial back seat, and still consider yourself a leader. You can't be quiet when the voice of reason needs to be heard. You can't sit idly as those around you take actions that may put themselves and others, especially the public, at risk. As Grossman (2010), a leading expert on communication inside organizations, so eloquently states: "You can't not communicate."

Step up and respond. That's what leaders do.

Defining Responsible Communication and Responsiveness

Before we get too far along, let's more fully define "responsible communication." Sending a mass email is *not* responsible communication. Neither is simply attaching your name to a blog entry, news release, or social media post. Delivering a speech or hammering through an agenda without adapting to the audience's reaction? Hosting weekend conference calls because you couldn't orchestrate effective conversations during the work week? These don't really constitute responsible communication, either.

What, then, is responsible communication? Answering that question requires dissecting the phrase into its two foundational words: responsibility, and communication.

Communication is an active process of two-way exchange. It's as much, if not more, about listening, monitoring, and responding, than it is simply talking, sending, or posting. Communication is never just one-way. If you think sending an e-mail message is communicating, you're wrong. That's nothing more than transmitting information. Likewise, telling someone what to do, or how to do their job, is not communicating. That's essentially just dictating orders.

Remember this important point: Communication is dialogue, not monologue. You communicate when you listen to someone *and* respond to the information they have shared with you in return. That listening process would ideally happen face-to-face, and in-person. But, you may also "listen" by carefully reading a report or message, by monitoring the body language of those attending a meeting or presentation, or paying attention to industry developments that are gaining attention with investors, in the news, or on social media. Responding involves clarifying your understanding of that information, and providing the sender or another appropriate stakeholder with meaningful interpretation and purposeful insight.

Chances are good that you truly communicate for at least a good portion of your day. But, it is not easy to focus, to stay tuned in, and to be fully responsive. There is so much information coming at us these days, and that is only compounded when you lead an organization, department, or team.

What about *responsible* communication, though? How does responsible communication differ from our traditional understanding of communication, as outlined above? Responsible communication means taking ownership of, and accountability for clear, candid, and consistent dialogue about values-based decisions. In other words, demonstrating daily that you sincerely care about ethical, moral, and social values, and all of the internal and external stakeholders who have a vested interest in your organization, institution, jurisdiction, or cause.

Let's say your company intentionally establishes some of its retail locations in urban neighborhoods that need gentrification. Doing so is not entirely consistent with your brand position, much of which is targeted at suburban households. Yet, as a company you value community and feel some sense of utilitarian duty to support the greatest good for all, even if these retail locations are not profitable and drag down overall company performance. Responsible communication would mean talking openly and candidly about the values-driven reasons for being in nontraditional markets, and for justifying losses that might otherwise mean higher wages for company employees, greater returns for investors, and a more impressive bottom line for financial news reporters to trumpet. This process would also involve listening intently to constructive feedback, taking to heart the concerns being expressed, and addressing

them as honestly as possible, regardless of whether the decision will ultimately be reversed or not.

Simply put, responsible communication means listening and responding to stakeholders, and truly living your values daily. This is the essence
of solid leadership. Sounds easy enough, right? Not exactly, as you likely
know from your own leadership experiences.

In business, we think of responsiveness as a competitive advantage, an
approach we take to customer needs, in order to stay ahead of the com-
petition (Martin and Grbac 2003). Applied to your leadership role, think
of responsiveness as an approach you take to stakeholder needs, in order
to maintain their commitment and enthusiasm. Let's consider a simple
example. It is easy to fire off a response to a subordinate's e-mail, or dismiss
an idea shared during a conference call or team meeting. When consider-
ing responsiveness as part of responsible communication and leadership,
though, that's not what should come to mind. Responsiveness, rather,
means being accessible and affirmative in the moment, while acknowledging that a fully realized opinion or decision will likely take more time and
input. Your primary job as a responsible communicator is not to plow
through conversations and e-mails, but rather to provide access to information, to acknowledge others' contributions, and to motivate stakeholders of all kinds to continue being advocates for your organization. Define
for others how responsive you intend to be, given normal circumstances,
and in times of escalation, emergency, or crisis; likewise, seek clarity about
how responsive others can be to your needs (Hyatt 2011).

Why Responsiveness Matters

In the ART of responsible communication, responsiveness is just as important as accessibility or transparency. What good is it to be approach-
able and open, if you don't respond to the needs coming your way? Yes,
responsible communication is truly an ART, more than a science. You
have to find courage in the moments, and to engage in a truly dynamic,
two-way fashion.

The process of voicing and fostering moral-based values requires considerable self-discipline and self-motivation (Gentile 2010). You can't just
react to a situation or opportunity from a technical or tactical view. You

are in a position of power and influence; you have to think things through end-to-end, and the beginning of that process should always be grounded in values. The trick is that the greater your responsibilities at work become, the more difficult this process becomes. You may have moved into management with the very best of intentions. You may have been incredibly thoughtful and responsive in those early days. But, the demands escalate as the days go by, and soon you are stretched so thin that there seems no or little opportunity for reflection, or for truly conscious values-grounded leadership and responsible, responsive communication.

Reflect for a minute now, though. Just think how many people rely on you every day. They can't do their best work, or even good work, without direction, approval, and/or a clear path. They also can't work for a greater good without someone reminding them of the values underpinning their work tasks. You owe it to your employees, and to yourself, to be fully engaged. That means giving voice to values, embracing criticism, addressing concerns, responding to pushback, and so much more. Yes, this kind of communication takes time and attention. But, the need for this investment is unquestionable. In a traditional examination of business success, responsiveness to customers is often identified as being essential (Martin and Grbac 2003). This book argues that responsiveness matters not only with customers and prospective customers, but with all of your internal and stakeholders. You must respond to those who have a vested interest in your organization. Fail to, and so, too, will your business likely fail, or, at the very least, seriously struggle.

Are values like responsibility and responsiveness truly that important, at least on a day-to-day basis? Studies suggest yes. Seems that what really holds the pieces together today for organizations, despite ever-increasing diversity and differentiation among stakeholders, is rich dialogue grounded in moral, social, and cultural values (von Groddek 2011). Consider a philanthropic gift by your company to a community organization that works with lesbian, gay, bisexual, and transgendered youth. There will be supporters and critics of such a donation, both within your organization and in the broader community. Such a donation may not have been fathomable a decade or two ago, and may still be considered inappropriate or even offensive by socially conservative citizens today. The reality is that the world is a much more diverse and inclusive place these days. You may even wonder how anyone could question such a charitable gift. Still, what's important is to ground decisions and communication in important discussions of moral, social, and/or cultural values. What does your company stand for today? How does this gift align with these values? How can you best share the news of this decision in a way that clarifies the values behind the decision, while keeping the door open to important dialogue with the community about these values and their relative importance? This does not mean making decisions by consensus, constantly bending to public criticism, or, worse yet, being unresponsive to stakeholders' input. What it means is knowing where your organization stands, value-wise, and then standing proudly yet not defiantly.

As a leader, you must embrace dialogue and debate, and stay responsive. Feedback from stakeholders is a sign they care. You want their passion, whether that's positive in spirit or more negative and constructive in nature. What you don't want in your stakeholders is apathy. Stakeholders must care about your organization, in order for growth to happen over time. Think of your company like a public school district; people invest their money and confidence in administrators and teachers, and they expect and deserve favorable outcomes in return. No matter the kind of organization you're managing, fostering dynamic, daily dialogue is key; it's also your responsibility as a values-based leader.

Act with Good Intent

It's no secret that with leadership comes power and influence. Nearly everything you do and say has some sort of impact. You may not think little things matter, particularly in day-to-day matters, but they absolutely do.

Let me share a story. Early in my career, I earned my first opportunity to write an executive speech for a chief executive officer. He was to deliver this speech to a national sales team, as part of an annual sales conference. This was his one chance per year to address all of the regional executives and their salespeople. The conference was roughly six weeks away, at the time the speechwriting process started.

To my surprise, the executive would not meet with me personally to discuss the speech or his expectations. I'm not sure whether he simply trusted me, or he felt this was a routine speech that did not require much of his personal investment. Regardless, I had to operate off handwritten notes from the CEO, provided to me by his administrative assistant. In turn, the CEO would not review an outline of the research I had conducted into how the sales team felt about certain pressing industry and organizational issues. What should have been a responsible communication process between a CEO and his speechwriter became nothing short of a communication breakdown.

Ultimately, the speech went through 16—yes, 16!—rounds of revisions. Was my writing not yet mature enough? Likely. Could I have been more assertive about getting face time with the CEO to discuss this speech? Perhaps. Still, every relationship is a 50–50 street. Half of the blame fell on this executive, who didn't ground in his behavior in the stated values of the organization, which included teamwork. He would not collaborate, and the process became so much more cumbersome than necessary. He selfishly cost the company an unnecessary amount of my time and, most importantly, put at risk his rapport with the sales team at this once-per-year opportunity to rally the troops.

The speech ultimately was delivered at the sales conference, and was met with positive response from those in attendance. The behind-the-scenes struggles didn't show through in the final delivery. It may come as no surprise, though, that this CEO is no longer a CEO. He wasn't one to take responsibility regarding communication or respond appropriately to subordinates' needs, and those were ultimately fatal flaws.

Even if you are not a CEO, you exercise considerable power and control every day—by what you share, how you share it, when you share it, and with whom. Never ever underestimate the power of your words and actions, as well as the power of your silence, distance, and unresponsiveness. How do you treat the people in your organization, especially those who are not anywhere near your rank in title? What values do you bring forth in how you conduct yourself at work?

Power can be used in subtle, yet highly impactful ways. Consider tobacco company Philip Morris and its public outreach in the 1990s. As health concerns and anti-tobacco activism rose among the public, the company worked to redefine the way in which it wished to be judged. Philip Morris pulled back from conversations about health issues, and shifted focus, instead, to philanthropy (Meyer and Kirby 2010; Murphy 2005;

Oliveira 2009). This was, in essence, a power play. By appealing to social values such as community and partnership, Philip Morris worked to shift the public conversation away from the health concerns associated with smoking. Have you ever shifted attention to appease others? Worse yet, have you shifted values to make a broader appeal? A responsible leader is clear and consistent on values, and communicates consistent with values-based decisions.

There have been instances when companies upload videotaped statements from executive spokespersons to the Internet, for public viewing, regarding allegations of internal corruption, embezzlement, and the like, rather than being directly responsive to news reporters. There may be legal restrictions at play, of course. However, the underlying strategy is to make the organization seem transparent and responsive, without having to answer reporters' questions and risk going off-message. Thus, in the absence of information and answers that the public most wants and needs, people jump to their own conclusions. That resulting perception can often be far worse than the truth. Putting the organization ahead of the public, then, isn't necessarily the right answer for anyone involved.

Do you ever try to avoid direct dialogue? Have there been situations in which you played up certain benefits or aspects, in turn drawing attention and focus away from perceived or real negative effects? That kind of leadership behavior is not inherently illegal or even necessarily unethical. However, there can be significant underlying concerns.

Your fundamental communication responsibility is not to protect ego, control messages, and dictate behavior. Rather, you should facilitate dialogue and help people feel safe speaking up and voicing their values. If members of your team feel strongly about what is right in a particular situation but don't feel confident acting on their convictions, you are failing them as a leader (Gentile 2010, xii).

Pretend you lead a software development firm. There are a few known bugs in a newly released product. You want to do right by customers, but reissuing the product now would be so costly. If you can simply hold off until the next scheduled update release, you will save your company significant money. Meanwhile, your service team is receiving more and more complaints. The service representatives might even be sharing their concerns with one another. However, for some reason, they do not feel confident recommending that a quick-fix update be released now, even though it seems obvious that customers are quickly growing disgruntled. What have you done, or not done, to create an environment where people do not feel confident raising their voices, especially when it comes to customers' needs and wants? What sort of retribution might they fear, should they openly speak their minds? How have leaders handled their feedback in the past?

Responsible communication is, ultimately, an obligation. In fact, some even define such communication as a contract between individuals. The ground rules include sincerity, relevance, continuity, clarity, prudence, tolerance, openness, prompt resolution, balance, and optimal timing (Dresp-Langley 2009). Can you fire on all of these cylinders all of the time? Likely not. However, you can make a concerted effort to respect as many of these guidelines as possible. A great one to start with is simply being open—open to conversation, open to feedback, open to ideas, open to criticisms.

What may happen if you violate the social contract between you and your employees and other stakeholders? Communication suffers, of course. However, there can be more serious and far-reaching potential impacts. You may impact or even abolish a broad sense of trust, and negatively affect individuals' self-confidence, particularly junior employees who do not share your hierarchical status or decision-making power (Dresp-Langley 2009). Communication is not dictatorship, after all; communication, especially the responsible kind, is dialogue.

Foster Responsiveness in Others

Executives who excel at communication are exceptional storytellers. They identify anecdotes from their own professional and personal lives, and use these stories to reflect and reinforce the core values of their organization. Of course, these anecdotes help endear these leaders to others inside, and outside of, the organization, by making them seem more real and down-to-earth. Stories often stoke a shared frame of reference, which makes it more comfortable for others to speak up and share their own experiences and insights.

But it's not just charismatic stories that excellent communicators share. They also craft compelling arguments about the direction of the organization, drawing on facts, industry analysis, and the link. Finally, these executives are conversational, they listen, and they improvise, responding to nonverbal cues such as signs of interest, boredom, confusion, and so on (Forman 2007). This means editing themselves as they speak, and adapting the story to the audience's reaction and perceived needs.

How many times have you led a meeting during which people are playing with their mobile devices, staring out the window or into space, having side conversations, or doodling on a printed agenda or handout? Don't feel bad. This happens to the best of us. But, what can you take from such experiences, looking at these situations from a lens of responsible communication? Rather than jabbering away about whatever you planned to discuss, why not simply ask people what they would prefer to hear about, or what is not resonating with them thus far? Better to spend two minutes clarifying the audience's needs than spending 20 minutes trying to fulfill your own.

What skills do you need to fashion yourself as a solid leader? Business executives consider integrity, communication, and responsibility among the 10 most important qualities or skills for today's business climate (Robles 2012). Integrity means having strong personal values, and consistently doing what is right. Communication involves listening, not just talking. And, responsibility means being accountable, reliable, resourceful, self-disciplined, and conscientious.

What role do values play in all of this? Organizations typically champion values when defining organizational identity, discussing and promoting social responsibility initiatives, or plotting future strategies (Murphy 2005; von Groddeck 2011). As a leader, you should be helping driving value-based communication—not just in these three areas, but, truly, in all aspects of your operations. This kind of leadership requires a fundamental understanding of the fact that responsible communication is never finished. There may not be immediate results, and the steps that helped address or resolve an issue today may not necessarily work down the road (Marken 2001). Communication is dynamic, and, as a leader, you must remain equally dynamic. Together with your stakeholders, mutually focus on important issues and value-based decisions, for they are the stories that truly matter.

Organizational environment, technology, roles, and other factors all impact communication leadership (Werder and Holtzhausen 2011). Such facets have an impact on adaptability and authority, especially when it comes to responsible communication. Research suggests that public relations leaders tend to serve as ethics counsel or corporate conscience within their organizations, but do so with little understanding or support from other executives (Bowen 2008). Before picking up this book, have you invested much time in better understanding the tenets of responsible communication? Have you partnered effectively with your corporate communications team, or ever thought about how to do so? Have you taken ownership for those aspects of communication clearly within your domain?

As a leader, you absolutely can make a difference when it comes to responsible communication with stakeholders inside and outside of your organization. The next few chapters will show you how.

Reflection Questions

- **Step up and respond. That's what leaders do.** Think of a few recent times when you have stepped up, rather than stay quiet or passive. What kind of response did this engender from others? How might you be more responsive as a leader?
- **Communication is dialogue, not monologue. You communicate when you listen to someone *and* respond to the information they have shared with you in return.** Would others consider you a good listener? Why or what not? In what ways could you become a more active, thoughtful listener?
- **Nearly everything you do and say has some sort of impact. You may not think little things matter, particularly in day-to-day matters, but they absolutely do.** Think back on the past few weeks or months. Can you think of a moment or two when you wish you would have conducted yourself differently? How about a moment or two that make you particularly proud of how you acted? What did you do or say in that moment that lets you know, deep inside, that you handled the moment responsibly?
- **Executives who excel at communication are exceptional storytellers.** They identify anecdotes from their own

professional and personal lives, and use these stories to reflect
and reinforce the core values of their organization. Can
you call to mind a powerful story from your own career or
personal life that would resonate with your employees? What
is it about that story that makes it so meaningful to you?
What's the lesson in that story for others?

- **Responsible communication is never finished.** There may
not be immediate results, and the steps that helped address
or resolve an issue today may not necessarily work down the
road. How well do you handle lack of closure? Uncertainty?
Continual change? What might you do to modify your
leadership style to help others navigate through some of these
modern-day professional challenges?

Responsible Actions

- **Understand "responsible communication"**—Take
accountability for clear, candid, and consistent exchange.
Demonstrate daily that you care about all of the internal
and external stakeholders who have a vested interest in your
organization, institution, jurisdiction, or cause. Listen and
respond to stakeholders, and truly live your values daily. This
process of voicing and fostering moral-based values requires
self-discipline and self-motivation.
- **Use your power for good**—Facilitate dialogue and help
people feel safe speaking up and voicing their values. If
members of your team feel strongly about what is right in a
particular situation but don't feel confident acting on their
convictions, you are failing them as a leader.
- **Foster stories that matter**—Drive value-based communication
in all aspects of your operations, with a fundamental
understanding that responsible communication requires
diligence and adaptiveness. There may not be immediate results,
and the steps that helped address or resolve an issue today
may not necessarily work down the road. Communication is
dynamic, and, as a leader, you must remain equally dynamic.

CHAPTER 3

Transparency

For several years, I worked independently and exclusively as a full-time consultant. If you have ever managed a similar business, or know someone who has, you understand the concept of transparency. Everything a consultant does and says is subject to scrutiny, and rightly so. Clients make a considerable investment when they affiliate with a consultant, and especially so when they share or hand over responsibilities to an independent consultant who lacks the backing or established track record of a big-name firm. Business is at stake, and so, too, is reputation.

This isn't really a story about me, though. This is a story about one of my friends, who is a serial entrepreneur. Her career is one series of high-minded, high-risk adventures after another. She has often-brilliant ideas, pulls the right team and sufficient resources together, gets the plane off the ground, and then moves on to the next challenge. She would never join a consulting firm; she's absolutely the captain of her ship, and happily and profitably so.

What does it take—beyond vision and a ton of hard work—to move so efficiently and effectively through the innovation process, like my friend does? Transparency. She's fully confident in herself, in what her team can do, and in facing any challenge that might come their way. She freely admits she is not perfect, and that mistakes may be made along the way. But, through it all, my friend remains transparent to her clients and colleagues. She's accessible and responsive, yes, but she's also open and candid—about whatever strategy is on the table, about the structure within which the strategy is being employed, and about herself, as an individual inspiring and guiding people, through strategy and structure, toward measurable results. Back home in South Dakota, we'd call her a straight-shooter.

There was a time, nearly a century ago, when the individual was seen as the center of business communication and corporate ethics. In the decades since, though, we have come to understand and appreciate that responsible, value-based communication involves project teams, departments, executives, and really everyone who has a vested concern in outputs and outcomes (DeKay 2011). The leader of such efforts, like my entrepreneurial friend, must proactively engage with stakeholders, being as fully accessible and forthright as possible. Too much is at stake, otherwise. In these challenging times, we put our trust and faith in leaders whose values we know, and, therefore, whose words and actions we can believe.

The word "transparency" has become a cliché in business. Let's look beyond that cliché, then, and examine specific leadership actions, in the spirit of transparency, that help build breed confidence and trust. First, though, we need to define transparency in the context of responsible communication.

Defining Transparency

Sharing information. Not having hidden agendas. Being forthright. These are some of the simple definitions that come to mind when we think of transparency. At an international conference on the subject, scholars proposed that a more precise of transparency involves two dimensions: being visible and being inferable (Michener and Bersch 2011). In the example of information or data, being visible would mean being easily located and complete; being inferable, then, would mean being thorough enough to draw verifiable inferences. How do these concepts relate to leadership and responsible communication? For argument's sake, let's play with the concept. As a leader, are you as visible as possible, and are you sharing a complete picture with your team or stakeholders? Likewise, is that picture robust and multidimensional enough in order for others to draw solid conclusions? In other words, being transparent in your communication as a leader might simply mean being forthcoming, sharing as much as you possibly can, and making sure that what you're sharing is infused with enough input in order to provide a complete picture.

Let's say you have been asked to sit in on a town hall meeting with customer service employees. Rumors are circulating that the service staff will soon be trimmed. There is some truth to that rumor, but there are several complexities and considerations that cannot yet be addressed with those who may be impacted. How do you approach such a conversation (and it should be a conversation, not a canned presentation)? First, you make the effort to attend that meeting, and to be fully engaged while there. You share as much information as you can, within legal and human resources constraints. And, as you answer questions and address concerns, you proactively remind those attending that the decision process is still in progress, and that nobody should yet draw any conclusions. You do your best to put people at ease, and to recognize that this is a difficult time. You are, in fact, there to listen to concerns and, to whatever degree you can, carry these concerns forward into the decision making. Will people get all the answers they want and need? No. But, they will get the sense that they are valued, that you take responsibility for what is happening, or what may happen, and that you understand or at least acknowledge the pain such a change might bring.

John Bernard, in his book *Business at the Speed of Now*, identifies seven rules for what he coins "total transparency." All seven rules are important, but specific to responsible communication, four of them carry exceptional weight: seek facts, not blame; speak the truth and respect fully; think organizationally, not departmentally; and engage fully (Bernard 2011). As a leader and a responsible communicator, you will arrive at your own working definition of transparency, one that fits your role, your values, your organizational culture, and your competencies. Keep Bernard's rules, and the principles from this chapter, in mind as you do; incorporate and integrate all that you can. The more transparent you can become, the more impactful your leadership will likely be.

Why Transparency Matters

Transparency can directly impact the bottom line. According to a 2011 Corporate Executive Board survey, organizations that worked to eliminate employees' fear or retaliation for honest feedback earned, on average, total shareholder returns of 7.9 percent, versus 2.1 percent for those organizations that did not (Bock 2012). Is there a guarantee that transparency will improve profitability, or even performance? Of course not. But, think of the good that may come, financially and otherwise, from improving your leadership transparency.

Conditions are tough for any organization, and seem to be getting tougher all the time. There is no doubt that organizations need transparent leaders who help build and manage reputation. In fact, when it comes to communicating about values-based issues like corporate social responsibility initiatives, the credible, reliable involvement of leaders has shown to be essential to fostering a positive organizational reputation (Jadhi and Acikdilli 2009). Transparency for leaders like you, then, involves being knowledgeable, engaged, and consistently involved or, at the very least, consistently open. Not making yourself transparent, especially with values-driven strategies, casts a dark shadow over otherwise good work being executed by the organization.

This book argues that the dynamic, ongoing dialogue you should be having with stakeholders is how corporate values and ethics will truly come to life. This give-and-take is the stuff of authentic relationship-building, true problem-solving, and tangible performance improvement (Llopis 2012). Failing to communicate and stay transparent may result in your employees taking unethical actions or changing their reporting standards (Halter and de Arruda 2009). Beyond the organization, your lack of transparency can send mixed or faulty signals to investors, policymakers, news reporters, and the general public. As a leader, you must sincerely put your values into action, and put your strengths to work.

Let's pretend your organization intends to exit a particular geographic market. You know customers in that area will be unhappy, and that the news media will be critical. If you have shareholders or other investors, they may get jittery. And, if you're in a regulated industry, you also have that consideration, too. This sort of exit process takes considerable time and fairly involved strategy. How do you maintain a spirit of leadership transparency when you know full well that the time will soon come to announce an end to that part of the business? You have to put your faith and trust in other leaders in your team. Be as transparent as you can with them, and, when you're finally at liberty to announce plans, notify and engage stakeholders as quickly and consistently as you can. Why? Because being transparent means stepping up, being visible, and providing multidimensional information so that people can draw solid conclusions.

Transparency is about showing respect for very real human concerns and needs. Transparency is about leading with dignity and character.

Put Your Strengths to Work

How do you best put your strengths to work, though, in terms of transparency and responsible communication? It's a tricky challenge, to be certain. One approach is simply to keep four considerations forefront in your mind: ethical intent of what is being considered, ethical means for realizing that objective, the responsible ways to communicate about the initiative, and, ultimately, the ethical outcomes (Tilley 2005). This model, the ethics pyramid, is how those who work in public relations incorporate ongoing ethical reflection and evaluation in their work. They think about the intent of decisions being made, they scrutinize the methods and processes by which certain decisions will be fulfilled, they determine the most consistent and fair way to communicate, and keep a watchful eye on end results, gauging whether values-based objectives were truly met or not. This process is not always linear, nor necessarily conscious. But, we know from corporate communication and public relations practice that this pyramid model is constantly in play.

You are not a full-time communicator, though. You have other priorities, other demands on your time, and certainly other skill sets. What should you do regarding responsible communication, and how can you help? More importantly, why should you care, when you have so many other obligations to fulfill?

Crises are often what draw leaders into communication. That is *not* leadership. Real leadership is acknowledging that, even in the most routine of times, you are often the most powerful person in a room or situation. Whatever you do and say—or don't do and say—sets the tone for everyone else involved in the situation, or who may ultimately be impacted by the situation. People take their cues from leaders.

In your aspiration to be a responsible communicator, the best move you can make is to start with your strengths top-of-mind. Are you a relationship-builder? A motivator? A pragmatist? Whatever your leadership style, be conscious of your underlying competencies. Perhaps your strength is industry knowledge. Or analytical thinking. Or emotional intelligence.

Whatever strengths define you, those are the strengths you should play on, and play up, as you communicate. They are the authentic you.

Granted, your communication style may not necessarily be the most effective for every situation. However, merely stepping up and being a solid, consistent leader—regardless of circumstances—is vital (Gentile 2010). Imagine that a colleague at work passes away unexpectedly, causing emotional ripples in the office and a very real hole, talent-wise, within the organization. The situation might make you uncomfortable; after all, you are human, just like your employees. But, you cannot ignore the situation or brush it off with disregard. You may not be one who is comfortable expressing emotions, but do the best you can. Be the person you are, and be that person consistently, in good times and bad. Lean on your personal values and those of your organization; look to them for inspiration in those times when the words don't come easily.

People need to know who you are and what you stand for, and they need to see you consistently live those values at work, and throughout diverse challenges. Being yourself, and being consistently active and responsive as a communicator, is the kind of authentic leadership that brings meaning to a tired word like "transparency."

Advocating Honesty 24/7

Of course, more communication doesn't necessarily generate or guarantee greater levels of trust among stakeholders. Corporations and other organizations have increasingly disclosed more information about social, ethical, and environmental performance, for example, but public trust has not grown accordingly (Dando and Swift 2003). At a corporate level, the link between transparency and accountability has to do with responsiveness and consistent improvement. That is, actions tend to speak louder than words. The same can be said of individual leaders. The more that leaders like you are consistently involved in communication, the better. Likewise, the more responsive you can be when issues arise, the better.

Let's imagine you manage emissions for a large factory located in a populated valley. Your business might make quarterly or even monthly reports about these emissions available to the public. Simply releasing this information will not necessarily win the public's support. The truth is that emissions are still happening, and no amount of communication is going to change that fact. What would really win the public's confidence is being as honest as possible about the environmental impacts, being responsive to the public's concerns, and making concerted efforts to reduce emissions, even in small increments, over time. This dynamic good faith effort will likely be more powerful, in terms of winning public support, than any amount of static reporting.

As a leader, you can apply this same approach to your own words and actions. Simply managing to the numbers, and rewarding or penalizing based on performance, will not significantly improve employee buy-in and spur organizational growth. What is more likely to drive morale and positive change is honesty about economic challenges and organizational circumstances, and responsiveness to employees' concerns and suggestions.

Just like organizations, their individual leaders must be seen as having integrity, respecting stakeholders, and being open and responsive in their communication efforts (Rawlins 2009). Being proactive, rather than reactive, helps prevent concerns the public might have about legitimacy and intent. Additionally, a proactive spirit help demonstrate an unwavering commitment to values (Arvidsson 2010).

Stay Accessible and Responsive

Remember that responsible communication is an ART—stay Accessible and Responsive while amping up your Transparency. Being consistent in your communication is, indeed, important for establishing legitimacy (Massey 2001). That's not just from a corporate perspective, but from the perspective of individual leadership, too. For example, Airbnb founder Brian Chesky handled all aspects of his business, including communication, in the startup's early days. He did so, admittedly, in order to manage consistency and make maximum impact (Carr 2014). But, even despite the best intentions, no leader can control things indefinitely, and that is especially true when it comes to communication. The leaders who practice responsible communication know that being consistent is far more important than trying to control or contain the communication process.

Indeed, change is continual in business. What is paramount to responsible communication is a solid understanding of issues management.

Any smart leader monitors issues and trends, and moves quickly to action as necessary. The problem comes when a leader assumes an issue or crisis has been resolved, because honestly, the "resolution" of an issue or crisis is really just the beginning of whatever the next phase might be (Jaques 2009). Managing issues, and advocating for responsible communication, comes with an acceptance that few issues are ever fully resolved. You must take a long view while staying responsive and decisive in the moment.

Take the case of a large-scale distribution center. Suppose an approved path for drivers to bring trucks to your facility may prove inefficient over time, for whatever reason. You could make a rerouting decision that's in your company's best interest, and disregard others' concerns. Ultimately, that decision you make in isolation will come back to bite you, assuming the new path has ramifications on traffic volume and movement, not to mention neighboring businesses, residences, and/or local laws or policies. A responsible communicator would monitor traffic issues and public complaints in the area, what competitors are doing in other markets to streamline deliveries, and other information that would help inform a values-based decision. There would also be considerable value in floating the proposed new route by stakeholders before moving ahead with implementation.

You absolutely should not wait for an issue to develop, or a crisis to unfold, to get involved in communication. As a leader, you should continuously monitor issues and trends, such as economic conditions, competitor performance, demographic trends, customer satisfaction, employee engagement, shareholder sentiment, or whatever might ultimately impact your business. As a responsible communicator, you should help identify and proactively address possible counter-arguments to your organization's performance or stance on important issues and indicators. Doing so can help curb perceived hypocrisy and negative attitudes (Wagner, Lutz, and Weitz 2009).

Where should you have learned the communication skills you need? Most business schools teach the competencies necessary for leaders like you to foster values and facilitate mutually beneficial activities with the community (Pies, Beckmann, and Hielscher 2010). It is your responsibility, though, to take these lessons to heart, and to live your values daily. Being a responsive and decisive leader is perhaps the ultimate contribution you can make to your business—and to society, as a whole.

Reflection Questions

- **In these challenging times, we put our trust and faith in leaders whose values we know, and, therefore, whose words and actions we can believe.** Who do you believe in? Who believes in you? What qualities and behaviors instill a solid sense of trust and confidence?
- **Being transparent in your communication as a leader might simply mean being forthcoming, sharing as much as you possibly can, and making sure that what you're sharing is infused with enough input in order to provide a complete picture.** How do you know when you're being transparent? And when you're not? What might you do to keep yourself in better check, so that you're staying as open and candid as you can possibly be?
- **Being proactive, rather than reactive, helps prevent concerns people might have about your legitimacy and intent.** What nags at you, as far as a situation or consideration that you haven't yet brought to the table with others? What's holding you back? How might you overcome those hurdles?
- **As a responsible communicator, you should help identify and proactively address possible counter-arguments to your organization's performance or stance on important issues and indicators.** What ventures or circumstances might cause your organization some problems? How can you bring different viewpoints to the table, in order to help affirm where your organization stands?

Responsible Actions

- **Put your strengths to work**—Real leadership is acknowledging that you are often the most powerful person in a room or situation. Whatever you do and say—or don't do and say—sets the tone for everyone else involved in the situation, or who may ultimately be impacted by the situation. Your best move is to start from your strengths. Your communication style may not necessarily be the most effective for every situation, but stepping up and being a solid, consistent leader regardless of circumstances is vital.

- **Advocate honesty 24/7**—Simply managing to the numbers, and rewarding or penalizing based on performance, will not significantly improve employee buy-in and spur organizational growth. What is more likely to drive morale and positive change is honesty about economic challenges and organizational circumstances, and responsiveness to employees' concerns and suggestions.

- **Be responsive and decisive**—You absolutely should not wait for an issue to develop, or a crisis to unfold, to get involved. As a responsible communicator, you should help identify and proactively address possible counter-arguments to your organization's performance or stance on important issues and indicators. Managing issues, and advocating for responsible communication, comes with an acceptance that few issues are ever fully resolved. You must take a long view, while staying responsive and decisive in the moment.

PART 2

Communicating Responsibly with Key Stakeholders

CHAPTER 4

Managers and Supervisors

The bulk of my professional experience stems from working within Fortune 250 corporations, and from collaborating directly with executives and the other leaders and employees within their respective business or support units. Administration, finance, human resources, legal, information technology, marketing, sales, service—my teams supported all of these areas, and more.

What proved most challenging, communication-wise, when working cross-functionally? You might have guessed: mergers, acquisitions, and joint ventures. Sure, rolling out new products or services was sometimes tough. But, most of those efforts involve leaders and teams who already know and trust one another. The sense of relationship that's already in place helps provide some degree of mutual trust and cooperation. That's not at all the case when it comes to merger, acquisition, or joint venture.

Want to witness people being really on-edge? Start working on a merger, acquisition, or joint venture behind closed doors, and observe how your fellow leaders, and especially those of the other organization, respond. Change rattles even the best of leaders, especially when that change might impact them personally. Negotiating for power, control, and longevity only exacerbates these nerves.

Having spent so many years in the financial industry, I have worked on more mergers, acquisitions, and joint ventures than I can recall. One particular experience sticks out more than any other memory, though. You will quickly appreciate the leadership lesson.

The acquisition in question was to be announced later in the week, and had been in a confidential planning process for months. Less than 48 hours before the internal and external announcements, which were to be closely synchronized, an urgent conference call for the members of the project leadership team was held. The senior sales and marketing executives within the company to be acquired were threatening to inform key vendors and mid-level managers on their side in advance of the announcement, or even convince their chief executive to pull their company out of the deal altogether. They used this leverage to force a midnight-hour renegotiation of compensation terms for themselves and their management teams, which inevitably opened the door to a host of further short- and long-term ripple effects, some of which had been planned for as contingencies, but many of which could not be remediated on such short order. Literally tens of thousands of dollars were burned in the final hours, as both parties scrambled to protect turf. Meanwhile, suspicion grew among employees in both organizations, and among members of the trade media and the investment community. Ultimately, the deal came together, but not without significant financial and reputational impact.

The reality is that this unnecessary situation was an ego play by a few irresponsible leaders of the company to be acquired. They were not leading with values. Key leaders from both companies had been involved in the due diligence and change management processes for months, all under signed confidentiality agreements. Values and principles had been clearly articulated at the outset. What changed in those final hours had nothing to do with value-based concerns.

From a communication perspective, we managed through this difficult situation as best we could, striving to be as accessible, responsive, and transparent as possible with managers, supervisors, employees, contractors, and other key stakeholders. The lesson, though, is that communication can only be as effective and responsible as the leaders involved. They set the tone. Likewise, you set the tone within your organization. Be upfront. Don't have hidden agendas. Never let power go to your head; people's lives and livelihood are at stake.

Take ART to heart: stay Accessible, Responsive, and Transparent. Your role, as a leader and a responsible communicator, is to empower others to help lead, regardless of their rank or title. Pontefract (2013), author of *Flat Army: Creating a Connected and Engaged Organization*, explains the modern leadership role this way: "Asking questions, involving people, connecting them to each other, creating a platform for their insights and ideas to make real impact—in other words, unleashing leadership behavior everywhere."

Commit to Shared Principles

As a leader, you have a responsibility to voice your values early and often—and every right to speak up when things don't seem fair or right. But, how much your personal wallet will be padded isn't a question of organizational values. There should be a higher calling, or at least a more altruistic purpose.

Most companies these days have clearly defined codes of ethics and/or principles (Murphy 2005). These documents mean nothing, though, if leaders do not take ownership and take these values to heart, through their daily words and actions. As a leader, you sign on to be involved in tough decisions, and to understand that your role is to move the organization, and not your personal agenda, forward.

What you do and how you act, particularly on issues and initiatives that are not yet employee or public knowledge, is pivotal. Gentile (2010) makes note in her book, *Giving Voice to Values,* of many things within our control that make it easier to speak and act on our values. Consider a few of these key factors:

- Start with questions rather than assertions.
- Secure more information to better inform your viewpoint.
- Appeal to shared purpose and values.
- Accept that managing conflict is simply part of a leader's job.
- Take difficult conversations offline, one-on-one, at a mutually convenient time and place.
- Enlist allies.
- Find win-win solutions.

What I know from the acquisition described earlier is that there would have been a much better way for the sales and marketing executives to conduct themselves. They could have asked more questions, rather than make assertions. They could have appealed to a shared purpose and values. They could have proposed a win-win solution, instead of making a selfish threat. They likely should have enlisted allies before making a midnight-hour bargaining threat. Waiting until the final hours like these two did, then making a power play out of the blue, is simply not values-based leadership, nor is it responsible communication.

Model Desired Behavior

Imagine that managing communication is your full-time job and your number-one responsibility. What competencies would find to be most important? Mid- to senior-level executives who work in public relations consider excellent leadership in their profession to involve strategic decision-making capability, problem-solving ability, and communication knowledge and expertise (Meng et al., 2012). They must have a compelling vision for communication, understand diverse forms of media and information systems, and develop and implement strategic communication plans.

Nobody expects you to act just like a corporate communications executive. However, you can model behavior that you desire to see in your peers, in your direct reports, and in all of the employees of your organization. The more you care about communication, the more people will care about communicating with you. It's really that simple.

First, you can develop a compelling vision by drawing on your experiences in decision making and problem-solving, and carrying those stories through in your various communications. Help others understand how and why you make certain decisions, and the values which inform those important choices. Second, you can and should communicate effectively in multiple ways. Face-to-face is the most powerful and meaningful, but that's not always possible, especially for a busy leader. Become adept at videoconferencing, hosting town halls, meeting with small groups, blogging on the company intranet and Internet, and so on. There are surely communication experts in your organization who can help expand your skills and reach, while connecting with stakeholders in the ways that are the most meaningful and efficient. Finally, take an active interest in communication plans, and/or how communication challenges are addressed as part of larger strategic plans. You should care, because in this digital age, any issue can spiral out-of-control very quickly.

Charismatic, human-oriented leaders tend to be perceived as the most communicative (De Vries, Bakker-Pieper, and Oostenveld 2010). Whether you consider yourself charismatic is not that important, though. What matters is that you make a real and human attempt to be actively engaged with stakeholders. Be supportive, assured, and precise, and you'll find that people will respond.

Hold Peers Accountable

Unless you are a sole proprietor, you are not alone in leading your organization. You need the support of your leadership peers, and all of you must share and promote fundamental values and principles. That's nonnegotiable for long-term organizational success and viability.

Why should you hold your peers accountable for responsible communication? Organizations must evolve over time, and change is exceptionally difficult for individuals. Effective change is more likely when people believe a change initiative is needed, has been designed appropriately, that organizational capability exists, that leaders believe in the change, and that the change will ultimately benefit them personally in some way (Torppa and Smith 2011).

Kotter (2005), the retired guru of change leadership, championed eight steps necessary for transformational change to happen effectively. The first three of these steps—establish a sense of urgency, form a guiding coalition, and create a vision—are essential elements of responsible communication. People need a burning platform in order to be moved to action. They need to see disparate leaders coalescing around an issue, to believe there is a concerted effort. And, finally, people need a clear vision in order to understand where change is headed, and what that change is necessary.

Kotter (2005) found that organizations could not skip or rush through steps and still hope to realize necessary change. The process takes considerable time, patience, and a sense of discipline. Similarly, organizations that make mistakes along the way lose momentum, and run the risk of never realizing the intended change.

Think about restructuring an organization. There must be an urgent and compelling need for such dramatic change. The right leaders have to get on board with the idea. And before any of the other change-related steps take place, there must be a clear vision, one that's values-based and truly compelling for people. Have you seen such a process bungled? What would have made such a transitional time unfold more smoothly?

What you should take from this chapter, is that if you do not voice your values and help drive communication, change will be exceptionally difficult for the organization and for all of the individuals who look to you for leadership. Commit to being a more responsible communicator, and hold your peers accountable for doing so, too. The organization will function more effectively and efficiently, and, ultimately, each of you should, too.

Reflection Questions

- **Accessibility—Charismatic, human-oriented leaders tend to be perceived as the most communicative.** Would you consider yourself charismatic? How might you bring more charisma to your approach? Charisma aside, in what ways can you make more real and human attempts to actively engage with stakeholders?
- **Responsiveness—As a leader, you have a responsibility to voice your values early and often—and every right to speak up when things don't seem fair or right.** How are you voicing your values at work? What specific examples could you cite as evidence?
- **Transparency—Help others understand how and why you make certain decisions, and the values which inform those importance choices.** Then, you can and should communicate effectively in multiple ways. How are you doing on both of these fronts? Do you regularly and explicitly discuss the values that factor into your decisions? Do you consciously strive to communicate in different methods, to ensure a consistent message reaches multiple stakeholders? How might you do better?

Responsible Actions

- **Commit to shared principles**—As a leader, you sign on to be involved in tough decisions, and to understand that your role is to move the organization, not our personal agenda, forward. What you do and how you act, particularly on issues and initiatives that are not yet employee or public knowledge, is pivotal.
- **Model desired behavior**—Help others understand how and why you make certain decisions, and the values which

inform those important choices. Communicate effectively in multiple ways; become adept at adapting your approach with stakeholders, as necessary. Take an active interest in communication plans, and/or how communication challenges are addressed as part of larger strategic plans.

- **Hold peers accountable**—Organizations must evolve over time, and change is exceptionally difficult for individuals. Effective change is more likely when people believe a change initiative is needed, has been designed appropriately, that organizational capability exists, that leaders believe in the change, and that the change will ultimately benefit them personally in some way.

CHAPTER 5

Employees and Contractors

It wasn't long into my managerial career before I faced the need to deliver news about layoffs. Granted, this   situation only impacted a few employees, but even one layoff can be difficult for a leader, and his or her team, to handle. The narrative can turn negative quickly, and, if the layoffs are not managed swiftly and carefully, the side effects can become grave and systemic.

How would you handle telling someone they have lost their job? And how would you tell the rest of the team? Maybe you have already been in these shoes. Or, if you are lucky, you have not yet had to face this possibility. The economy swings up and down, and, given enough time in one industry, proverbial blood will one day be on your hands, too, whether you want that responsibility or not. This is all part of leadership and business, for better or worse.

Chances are I will never forget the morning I had to personally deliver layoffs for the first time. Driving to work, I made a point of thinking through the decisions I had made in partnership with my executive team and with human resources. I thought about the values that factored into the decision-making process, and how I would best highlight these values in each conversation while giving each individual his or her deserved respect. Repeatedly, I practiced the words in my head while fighting back the heaviness in my heart.

The individual conversations went as well as possible. Gratefully, I had done the right amount of sifting through the options, justifying the decision with values clearly in mind, and preparing for the face-to-face notifications.

What did not seem to go as well were the days following those individual notifications. Yes, I had met with the other members of the team shortly after the individual notifications, to make sure everyone was aware of what was happening, and to address concerns as best I could. But there is only so much that can be said about how and why one individual's employment is terminated, while another's is not. And, in the absence of clear, candid, and consistent communication, the rumor mill runs rampant. That's exactly what happened in this situation. Rumors flew. But then, a week or so after the layoffs, several team members approached me individually, and in confidence, to thank me for being accessible, responsive, and as transparent as possible during this challenging time. I drove home at the end of that week with a smile on my face, knowing that my words and actions *do* matter and *do* make a difference.

To this day, I find layoffs among the most difficult form of communication a leader must handle. You are handcuffed by all of the necessary restrictions governing employment law. Keeping morale and engagement afloat among employees, despite these very real hurdles, can be incredibly tough.

Leaders do the best they can in these situations, or at least they should. And that's not just with layoffs, of course, but with all sorts of changes and challenges within an organization. For, without change, there would be no growth—and perhaps no survival, either. It is imperative for the organization that you personally embrace change, and know how to leverage the ART of responsible communication to keep employees engaged and productive.

Listen and Respond in Person

If you're a parent or guardian, aunt or uncle, or simply know someone with children of their own, you know that there is no problem getting kids to talk. In fact, getting children to be quiet is usually the difficult task! Children are usually uninhibited and outspoken; they are usually very clear about what they need and want. What happens to us, then, between childhood and adulthood? Why is it so hard to have candid conversations at work, and in other aspects of our lives?

Of course, adults are not children. We have taken on demanding responsibilities, have assumed emotional burdens, and have gathered years of experience with being misunderstood, judged, offended, hurt, ashamed, ridiculed, ostracized, and ignored by others. The path from childhood teaches us much about ourselves, and perhaps even more about others. We learn to temper our thoughts and feelings, we learn to muffle our voices, we learn to keep our ideas and emotions largely to ourselves. This process happens socially and emotionally at the playground, day care center, school, house of worship, and, ultimately, at work.

As a leader, how can you go about undoing years of psychological and emotional conditioning? In her book *Giving Voice to Values*, Gentile (2010) notes that there can be great value in simply talking at work about topics that are traditionally difficult to talk about in the workplace. For example, has someone on your team battled cancer? With that individual's permission, did you then talk openly with the team about what was happening? How the treatment might affect the individual and the work unit? What you all could do collaboratively to make this process as painless as possible for everyone involved?

As a leader, you have the power to open up natural dialogue, without having to make blanket decisions, declarations, or judgments (Gentile 2010). Simply by sparking conversation, you put others at ease, and help them feel more willing to raise their own voices. You demonstrate that you value hearing diverse thoughts and opinions, and that, regardless of the situation at hand, there is always time and space for candid conversation.

Of course, there is a time and place for group discussion, and for private conversation. Confidential, personal, and/or sensitive information is best handled face-to-face and one-on-one. Face-to-face communication is not always feasible, of course, but one-on-one communication usually is. A discreet phone call, when necessary, can be as personal and meaningful as a face-to-face conversation, especially when time and/or distance don't allow for a personal meeting Use your best judgment, but always, always, always try to personalize your approach when the message is of a sensitive nature.

Other information—especially straightforward information about project updates, meeting details, policy changes, systems issues, and so on—is usually most productive and even imperative to deliver via e-mail, to ensure everyone receives the same details and at the same time (Kupritz and Cowell 2011). Be careful, though. What you consider benign, someone else might consider controversial. A good rule of thumb is to rarely rely on sending e-mail as your only form of communication. Bundle that with personal interaction, group discussion in a regularly scheduled team meeting, and/or a presentation to a department or project team. Your goal is always to ensure that there's an invitation for open dialogue, and that you have the opportunity to listen to feedback and respond in real-time. Your colleagues are people, not robots. They have very real and very human thoughts and feelings. As their leader, you owe them your time and attention.

Let's imagine, for illustrative purposes, that there is a business reason to move people among cubicles, or perhaps even among buildings. This is a simple decision that could be communicated via e-mail, right? Yes. However, think of yourself and your own attachment to your office space. There's a comfort and assuredness that comes with knowing those who surround you, and with being in a location that's familiar. How about posting the same details to the company intranet, to make sure everyone knows what is happening, and is receiving the same message. That's better, right? Perhaps. Still, there is a better way: tap your front-line managers to deliver the message, and to talk through concerns with those involved, either as a group and/or with individuals. The idea, of course, is to create time and space for dialogue. You want employees to stay engaged; therefore, you want their feedback, whether that's positive or constructive. Either way, you are going to eventually need to address people's concerns. Do that before the grapevine goes to work, or grumbling begins in earnest. Be responsible, and open up fruitful dialogue as early as possible.

Moving employees is a relatively easy challenge. There isn't a great deal of sensitivity, nor is there much room for debate. What if your business fails an audit, though? How about if an employee is accused of sexual harassment? What if one of your company's delivery drivers accidentally runs over and critically injures a small child while on his or her route? What if a violent storm damages one of your operations centers, as well as the homes of several employees who live near that center? Unfortunately, crises of all sorts can and do develop. Some crises may be addressed openly; others, like the audit or harassment case, typically come with legal constraints that prohibit open communication. It is your responsibility as a leader to know and understand what issues you can address openly, and then to foster responsible communication. If you don't know your organization's policies, or you can't recall some of them, reach out to your human resources partner.

Rarely can you clam up altogether about a crisis. For most crises, in fact, the advice is to communicate quickly, accurately, and repeatedly with all stakeholders, including both internal audience and external audience, which encompasses news reporters (David 2011). You never want employees, vendors, or investors to find out about a crisis from news media, social media, or off-line word-of-mouth. You want employees to hear the news directly from you, or from another leader in your organization.

Is it always possible to prevent employees from hearing news from outside sources? No, not in this day of rapid-fire dissemination via digital technology. You and your leadership peers should do your best, though, to keep a clear, consistent dialogue going, both within the organization and outside of the organization. "No comment" is not acceptable. People have questions and concerns; they deserve answers. And, with employees, the more aware and engaged they are, the better ambassadors they can be for the organization. Arm them with information, and they can help spread the word, so that you don't have to carry the burden all alone.

Suppose you are a senior executive for a holding company of entertainment properties, including a large and popular amusement park that draws visitors from across the nation and around the world. Your property offers a unique thrill ride similar to that of a competing park, yet the rides were designed and installed by different engineering firms. A tragedy happens at the competing park, but you and your fellow leaders determine there is no risk to your patrons, and continue to keep your own, similar ride in operation. Naturally, visitors and prospective visitors to your park have concerns, and questions escalate. Is it enough to post a short notice on your website, and perhaps push a similar message out to the public, via news media and social media? Absolutely not. Provide all of your colleagues with ample information, and offer guidance on how they should respond to visitors' concerns and questions. One-on-one communication is the most powerful and meaningful form of communication, particularly in the face of tragedy. Treat your employees with respect, so that they, in turn, can demonstrate that same level of caring and attention to customers.

Foster a Dynamic Culture

We tend to think of employee engagement when a change or crisis unfolds. Whether we have paid employees sufficient attention before is not the question most leaders ask themselves. Their concern is this: What can I do right now to make sure people stay on task? That's an awfully selfish approach to leadership.

One of the most important roles you play within your organization is that of cultural champion. You should be doing something, or perhaps even many things, every day to help shape the kind of culture your organization needs to survive and thrive long-term. Heading straight to your office, jumping in and out of meetings, keeping your eyes focused on a computer monitor, tablet, or smart phone? Those are not leadership behaviors; they are task-oriented actions that selfishly focus on your day and your own needs.

A cultural champion tries to make the work environment as dynamic as possible for everyone involved. This means actively engaging with people, to understand what they need and want in order to do their jobs better, and to feel more satisfied and valued at work. There is rarely a one-size-fits-all solution. You will need to use different types of communication methods with different people; remain open and authentic when doing so; and report back to them on progress made in specific areas of concern or interest (Tucker 2013).

You may or may not be familiar with leader-member exchange (LMX) theory. Traditionally, we have looked at leadership from the point-of-view of the leader, or of the follower and the environmental context. LMX theory, though, acknowledges that a leader has different relationships with different followers (Northouse 2010). Some followers are the out-group, or the ones whose relationships with the leader are based on little more than the employment contract. Others are the in-group, or the ones whose relationships with the leader have become more personal and dynamic. Your responsibility isn't to ensure that every one of your followers becomes part of the in-group; in fact, that's not even feasible. There will likely always be some out-group members.

You do have a responsibility, though, to avoid creating an environment where followers, especially those in the out-group, feel apprehension about raising their voices. The reality is that this sense of apprehension among followers has greater impact on LMX quality than your communication style or your communication competence (Madlock et al. 2007). What can you do to ease apprehension? Get to know each of your followers as a person, as best you can and understanding that for some workers, developing a more personal relationship with one's leader is not at all desired. Still, you can work to become more aware of how each of your followers like to operate and communicate, and then stay mindful of these differences as you communicate. You may need to adapt your delivery in certain situations, or you may need to try a mix of communication methods to make certain that everyone in your team feels at least some degree of comfort with raising their voice.

LMX quality has a strong impact on employees' satisfaction with interpersonal, group, and organizational/enterprise-wide communication (Mueller and Lee 2002). That means how you conduct yourself as a leader, day-in and day-out, impacts how employees perceive personal feedback, supervisory communication, co-worker communication, organizational integration, corporate communication, and the overall organizational climate. Their perception of you shapes their reality of nearly every aspect of interaction and information-sharing at work. What you do, and especially what you don't do, does make a difference.

Consider this simple example. You like to exercise, and roughly one-third of your team likes to workout, as well. You may all take advantage of a corporate gym, or perhaps belong to nearby facilities. Regardless, being active is important to you, and to them. Naturally, conversations will happen about fitness regimen, nutrition, treating sore muscles, competing in local races, and so on. These simple, human connections start to create a special connection between you and certain employees. Other employees who do not enjoy exercise, or simply prefer not to talk about such parts of their life at work, don't get to share these moments with you. They may seem small and insignificant, but over time they create a human bond. Some of your followers will feel more connected to you, and special; others simply will not.

Take to heart another example. You have children, and most of your employees do, as well. A few of the people on your team, though, do not. You can imagine what happens each time a baby shower is announced, or details of a youth soccer match are discussed. Most employees feel part of the in-group, but a few do not. Now, what happens when those with children regularly leave the office at or before the end of the day, to shuttle kids to and from day care, school, activities, and so on? And what if those employees without children are quietly expected to cover for those who are parents? Does your company have a work-from-home policy for parents with sick children? Or, are those parents required to take vacation time? These are just some of the many questions and issues that arise when we start to pay attention to the very real and very meaningful differences between employees. What if one of the employees without children happened to be primary caregiver to an elderly parent? Would that change things?

You no doubt have support from human resources and other areas to work through policy and policy implementation issues. Still, you should strive to responsibly communicate with all of your employees. That means making a concerted effort to keep an open dialogue flowing with each employee, regardless of differences. Acknowledge what each person values and enjoys, the responsibilities he or she has outside of the office, and the like. As Gentile suggested, just starting the dialogue is often the sparkplug for engagement.

This may come as no surprise but the energy and motivation you put into employee relationships has proven to have a positive, significant impact on work attendance (Mayfield and Mayfield 2009). Over time, the responsible communication you foster with each individual employee may also help improve productivity, performance, and retention, as well.

As you proactively work to foster a dynamic culture, you must also appreciate generational differences. We often talk about Millennials, for example, as having an attitude of entitlement, because they place high value on leisure time and personal rewards. Does this mean Millennials are lazy? Not necessarily. As a generation, they truly want work to be meaningful, and part of this sense of meaning involves being in a culture that is rewarding and fun (Schullery 2013). Does this mean you need to offer more incentive bonuses to employees, or host wheelbarrow races down the aisles of your office? However, you should again be in tune with differences—be they generational or otherwise. Adapt your communication approach and your leadership style as best you can. Most importantly, have honest dialogue with each employee about what is important to him or her. Generational, cultural, and other differences do not apply universally, after all. Don't assume you know and understand; ask, or at least invite a conversation.

Finally, understand that employees may not appreciate your efforts to communicate more intently. They may find your behavior to be insincere or uncertain. In the case of corporate philanthropy, for example, employees tend to view corporate giving from a values-based foundation, but tend to resist corporate rationalization of strategic philanthropy (Smith 2012). What you might take from this example, should there be any linkages, is the importance of demonstrating a commitment to values. You might simply remind employees that you value honesty, and that honest conversation will not be met with resistance or retribution. They may not believe you at first, especially if this is not the kind of communicator you have been in the past. Assuming your actions stay consistent with your words, though, you should win more traction with employees over time.

Drive True Organizational Change

Keeping employees engaged is one challenge. Quite a different challenge is leading employees through organizational change, and truly driving that process. As noted earlier in this chapter, that leadership process begins by having employee conversations, especially ones with difficult topics or messages, in a one-on-one setting if you can, remaining calm, addressing the issues in question without passing judgment, and listening closely to feedback (Gentile 2010).

Indeed, the more you can do now to foster a dynamic, supportive climate should help dramatically when the time comes for organizational change, or when a crisis inevitably occurs. Continuous efforts by leaders to improve communication and ease employees' apprehension have been shown to result in more positive employee behaviors and less negative employee feedback during times of corporate crisis (Mazzei, Kim, and Dell'Oro 2012).

Moreover, a culture with leaders that model and encourage positive behavior can influence how employees interpret traditionally "bad news" messages. Employees in this kind of culture are resilient and optimistic when "bad news" hits, and they tend to focus on organizational strengths, rather than whatever threat is at hand (French and Holden 2012). This positive mindset starts with positive, values-based leadership, and responsible communication.

You have learned a bit about how to foster a healthier climate for employee communication and engagement, even during times of crisis. But, what about actually driving organizational change? How does responsible communication play into this process?

Just knowing your personal values, and the organization's values, isn't enough. Nor is staying true to those values, and being clear, candid, and consistent in your communications. The reality is that, in order to truly drive change, you may need to orchestrate a series of conversations with particular allies and audiences, in order to secure buy-in and support (Gentile 2010).

Let's say that your company, which has nationwide distribution, has decided to focus on its most profitable markets, and pull out of markets in the Upper Plains and the Southwest. All impacted employees will have the option to relocate, or to take a severance package. Sales, systems, service, and shipping teams will all need to revise workflows. You manage logistics for the company, and your job is to drive this change. It's not just the two geographic markets, and the employees within those markets, who will be affected. Nearly every employee in the company will feel the changes, in one way or another. Can you simply work with a small cross-functional team to implement the change? No. In fact, you will need to talk candidly and confidentially first with leaders of each functional area, to ensure their support, hear their concerns, and develop plans that mitigate those concerns. Only then will you be able to ask for support, and for a dedicated colleague to serve on your project team. And, all of that has to happen long before you hold the first project team meeting.

As always, your responsibility is to foster responsible communication. That means keep values first and foremost in your mind, and the minds of those from whom you are trying to garner support. That means talking honestly about the values that are driving this decision, and how this large-scale organizational change will help bolster organizational values for the long-term. That also means making sure each step in the communication and change process involves dialogue, and not simply dictating of orders. You may have a very clear end game in mind, and you may not be able to waver from that end game. How you and the organization get there, though, is certainly open for interpretation. You have a responsibility to ask questions, to listen, and to remain adaptive.

Reflection Questions

- **Accessibility—Simply by sparking conversation, you put others at ease, and help them feel more willing to raise their own voices.** You demonstrate that you value hearing diverse thoughts and opinions, and that, regardless of the situation at hand, there is always time and space for candid conversation. How have you demonstrated this kind of accessibility? What kind of reaction did that evoke?
- **Responsiveness—Making a continual effort to improve communication and ease employees' apprehension tends to result in more positive employee behaviors and less negative employee feedback.** Have you found this to be true in your own experience? What specific instance(s) do you recall? What lessons can you carry forward to future challenges within your organization?
- **Transparency—Responsible communication involves talking honestly about the values that are driving decisions, and how organizational changes will help bolster organizational values for the long-term.** Do you make it a habit to bring values into discussions with colleagues? How can you help people better understand how a particular change will help the organization better live its values?

Responsible Actions

- **Listen and respond in person**—By sparking conversation, you put others at ease, and help them feel more willing to raise their own voices. You demonstrate that you value hearing thoughts and opinions, and that, regardless of the situation, there is always time and space for conversation. Of course, confidential, private, personal, and/or sensitive information is best handled face-to-face and one-on-one. While face-to-face communication is not always feasible, one-on-one communication usually is. A discreet phone call, when necessary, can be as personal and meaningful as a face-to-face conversation, especially when time and/or distance don't allow for a personal meeting. Use your best judgment, but always, always try to personalize your approach when the message is of a sensitive nature.

- **Foster a dynamic culture**—You should be doing something, or perhaps even many things, every day to help shape the kind of culture your organization needs to survive and thrive long-term. A cultural champion tries to make the work environment as dynamic as possible for everyone involved. This means actively engaging with people, to understand what they need and want in order to do their jobs better, and to feel more satisfied and valued at work. This is rarely a one-size-fits-all conversation, though. Make accommodations to tailor communication to individuals and their unique differences and preferences.

- **Drive true organizational change**—The more you can do now to foster a dynamic, supportive climate should help dramatically when the time comes for organizational change, or when a crisis inevitably occurs. Continuous efforts by leaders to improve communication and ease employees' apprehension have been shown to result in more positive employee behaviors and less negative employee feedback during times of corporate crisis. Moreover, a culture with leaders that model and encourage positive behavior can influence how employees interpret traditionally "bad news" messages. Employees in this kind of culture are resilient and optimistic when "bad news" hits, and they tend to focus on organizational strengths, rather than whatever threat is at hand. As always, your responsibility is to foster responsible communication. That means keep values first and foremost in your mind, and the minds of those from whom you are trying to garner support. That means talking honestly about the values that are driving this decision, and how this large-scale organizational change will help bolster organizational values for the long-term. That also means making sure each step in the communication and change process involves dialogue, and not simply dictating of orders.

CHAPTER 6

Investors and Regulators

One of the most rewarding assignments of my career involved promoting homeownership among Native Americans, and, more specifically, the first-ever financing of tribal land in the United States, by a financial institution. Until that point, such a financing arrangement had not been legally possible. This initiative involved the federal government, state governments, tribal nations, individual homeowners, my employer, and a host of other partners. There was profit potential, of course, but underlying this effort was a clear corporate commitment to strong moral, social, and cultural values. We were helping tribal members borrow money to build and own property on tribal lands, for the first time in American history.

Certainly, I learned a lot about tribal heritage, government regulations, and alternative financing models during this project. What I also learned, though, is the power of such a story to investors and policymakers. A media relations manager and I had traveled to remote areas, meeting with tribal officials, bank representatives, federal and state officials, and, of course, the borrowers. We had developed a fairly straightforward strategic communication plan, with a focus on generating news coverage and informing our employees. What I had not expected was for this story to ultimately make its way, along with a full-color, full-page photograph, in the corporate annual report.

As a leader, you have an opportunity—and, yes, a responsibility—to capture and share meaningful stories that will help your organization, your investors, your community or communities, and the public. My mind had originally been solely on news releases, a press conference, media interviews, and a few write-ups for internal newsletters and intranet sites. I had not thought at all how this story so strongly reflected corporate values, as well as a corporate push to find untapped and potentially profitable markets. There really was a good story here, not only for tribal nations and Main Street, but for government officials and Wall Street, too.

Your primary responsibility is likely not investor relations or public affairs. In fact, due to strict regulations, you should not be communicating directly with investors or analysts, unless that is a defined part of your responsibility, and you have been trained how to do so (Murrey 2013). But, you can still contribute to investor communications indirectly. What are you and your team working on that might make a story that resonates with investors or policymakers? Do some of your initiatives and results reflect particularly strongly corporate values, as well as social, moral, and cultural values? Who can you engage to help capture and share these stories for your corporate communications team? After all, the more your organization can attract investor and regulator support, the more your business can expand and do even more good.

Responsible communication, when it comes to investor relations and public affairs, involves staying mindful about the work your team is doing, and how that supports corporate, social, moral, and/or cultural values. And, while you will likely not be handling analyst calls or lobbying duties yourself, you can become a partner in these efforts, funneling stories and metrics to the appropriate teams.

Let's look at a few ways to get involved.

Keep Pace with the Market

Whatever your functional area, you should be paying attention to industry trends and particularly analysts' and policymakers' opinions. Let the Internet do the work for you. Multiple different browsers, news sites, investment sites, and government sites allow you to subscribe to RSS feeds or, better yet, set up customizable alerts that automatically push headlines and stories to you, via email, however frequently you desire. You can set up alerts for multiple different issues and topics, and at the very least those alerts should cover your industry, your organization, and/or your functional area within the organization. It takes just a few minutes to scan these alerts; doing so is a rudimentary, yet helpful, method of environmental scanning and issues monitoring.

When it comes to the market, be aware that investors tend to react most enthusiastically to news items regarding new customers, completion of acquisitions, strategic long-term decisions, and nontechnological alliances (Cuellar-Fernandez, Fuertes-Callen, and Lainez-Gadea 2010). News about new or upgraded products is generally of less interest. In my example, the financing of property on tribal land involved new customers, a strategic long-term decision, and nontechnological alliances. This story had the elements that told a strong story of confidence, innovation, and growth to investors and policymakers.

Investor relations and public affairs are claimed as specializations of public relations, but they are not always perceived as such. The Public Relations Society of America and the National Investor Relations Institute surveyed their respective members, though, and found that investor relations executives conduct their work in very much the same way as corporate communication executives, with a consistent tendency toward two-way, symmetrical communication (Kelley, Laskin, and Rosenstein 2010). The takeaway is that basic tenet of responsible communication: we should be creating and encouraging mutually helpful discussions with investors and policymakers about values-based issues and decisions.

You see more and more of this mindset when it comes to Fortune 500 websites. Their online newsrooms have increased their presence over time, and more dialogue-generating stories and components are available now, to stimulate journalists' interest and use in news stories (Pettigrew and Reber 2010). What initiatives do you lead that might make good fodder for the corporate website, annual report, analyst calls, or lobbying?

Answer the Tough Questions

A mistake you might make is to assume that capturing and/or relaying a story is enough, when it comes to helping investor relations and public affairs efforts. The public and investors have grown increasingly skeptical and cynical. This has been particularly true when it comes to corporate social responsibility. Investor relations experts have been increasingly moving from a "broadcast" approach to much more of an interactive, two-way, relationship management process (Hockerts and Moir 2004). Analysts and policymakers are increasingly asking tough questions, as they should. What you should do is think about how you might help answer those tough questions.

Why is this important? Increasingly, at least from an investor relations perspective, corporate-driven communication is perceived as having as much, if not more, value than information conveyed via news media or other means (Penning 2011). Presumably, the direct method of communication, and the promise of two-way dialogue between analysts/investors and the corporation, fosters a sense of real value to those who want to know more.

Your subject matter expertise could prove particularly valuable. Are you funneling information for analyst calls, quarterly and annual reports, and lobbying efforts? Does that information include quantitative metrics, informative graphics, and/or digital images, along with meaningful anecdotes, direct quotations, and other narrative? Are there questions you frequently face? Could you or your team develop these into an FAQ? Have you thought of offering to sit in on an analyst call or be part of a lobbying effort? Remember, you have important stories to share, but you also could benefit from valuable feedback, criticism, and dialogue.

Look Ahead, Mitigate Risk

The old coaching adage applies to your role as a responsible communicator: defense is the best offense. That means anticipating counter-arguments to the stories and successes you wish to share inside your organization and with the public. Your personal values, or those of your corporation, may not necessarily be values shared or respected by your stakeholders, including investors, analysts, and policymakers. More specifically, the decisions your organization chooses to put forth may not be perceived as being in line with your stated values, and/or with the moral, social, or cultural values of the people and communities you serve.

As you set up online alerts and keep an eye on industry trends and issues, pay particular attention to criticisms and pushback. What pain points might your business face, if it pursues a certain path? How does perception differ from what you know is reality? How are values being lost in the message, or misunderstood in translation?

Thinking proactively, in this case, means you'll want to think more defensively—at least in your head, if not yet verbally. Every decision you make or help champion comes with trade-offs and downsides. Be honest about these concessions; their human, financial, and environmental impacts; and the perceptions they may generate from those who are not involved in the decision-making process.

Smart lawyers think ahead and mitigate risks. You should do the same, as often as you possibly can.

Reflection Questions

- **Accessibility—Responsible leaders stay mindful about the work their teams are doing, and how that work supports corporate, social, moral, and/or cultural values.** They engage themselves, however they can, and they champion these efforts. What projects are you personally getting behind? Do the teams involved know you're a champion for them? How? What can you do to help their efforts, and leverage their good for the greater good of the organization or industry?

- **Responsiveness—Leaders shouldn't be on the sidelines, especially when it comes to matters of company ownership and regulation.** You should be creating and encouraging mutually helpful discussions with investors and policymakers about values-based issues and decisions. What comes to mind when you think of issues and decisions that should be proactively discussed with investors and regulators? How do values play into these decisions and discussions? What would the ultimate benefit be of providing more values-based context to investors and regulators, and to other stakeholders, as well?

- **Transparency—The decisions your organization chooses to put forth may not be perceived as being in line with your stated values, and/or with the moral, social, or cultural values of the people and communities you serve.** How will you handle such a situation, or how have you handled similar situations in the past? How might you help prepare others in your organization, especially managers and supervisors, for such difficult conversations?

Responsible Actions

- **Keep pace with the market**—Whatever your functional area, you should be paying attention to industry trends and particularly analysts' and policymakers' opinions. When it comes to the market, be aware that investors tend to react most enthusiastically to news items regarding new customers, completion of acquisitions, strategic long-term decisions, and nontechnological alliances. You should be creating and encouraging mutually helpful discussions with investors and policymakers about values-based issues and decisions.

- **Answer the tough questions**—Analysts and policymakers are increasingly asking tough questions, as they should. Think about how you might help answer those tough questions. Your subject matter expertise could prove particularly valuable. Have you thought of offering to sit in on an analyst call or be part of a lobbying effort? Remember, you have important stories to share, but you also could benefit from valuable feedback, criticism, and dialogue.

- **Look ahead, mitigate risk**—Anticipate counter-arguments to the stories and successes you wish to share inside your organization and with the public. Your personal values, or those of your corporation, may not necessarily be values shared or respected by your stakeholders, including investors, analysts, and policymakers. Every decision you make or help champion comes with trade-offs and downsides. Be honest about these concessions; their human, financial, and environmental impacts; and the perceptions they may generate from those who are not involved in the decision-making process.

CHAPTER 7

Reporters and Editors

On the first day of my first corporate internship, which was with an industry-leading manufacturer, the media relations director handed me a news release and a list of trade media. My task was to call each of the editors and reporters on the list—more than 300 of them, from New York City to Los Angeles—and pitch them on a new product being launched across the United States. Before that day, I had not ever talked one-on-one with a news reporter.

Has your introduction to media relations been similar? I certainly hope not. However, few executives receive the background, briefing, and coaching they need to be truly successful as spokespeople. There can be an assumption that, given your title, you can talk to anyone effectively about any topic. That may be true in most situations, but working with editors and reporters brings with it unique challenges. Their agenda is usually not the same as yours, and a power struggle can ensue. Since they own the distribution channel, you are typically without much leverage. You have to really know what you are doing, and how to get the kind of coverage that's both accurate and fair.

My initial experience with pitching a news story—or "smiling and dialing" as we called it back in the day—did not go particularly well. I had a news release in front of me for reference. I had the right contacts at my fingertips. And, I had the faith and confidence of my supervisor. What I did not have was industry expertise or spokesperson training. The product launch was actually more of a product relaunch, with just a few minor technical tweaks. The media relations director knew this when giving me the assignment. If I could gain any media coverage, that would be a win. If I could not gain any coverage, no harm would be done—except to my ego. That assignment, as you can imagine, had one clear outcome:

a bruised ego for a university student who thought he could conquer the world. You sometimes don't succeed in business, I learned, even when you're trying.

Trying isn't enough when it comes to working with the news media. Talking to a reporter can be stressful and tenuous, even when you are well prepared. Regardless, a big part of responsible communication is owning the role of company spokesperson, and addressing the public's need for information. It helps to know the basics of media relations, and to keep in mind the values you wish to espouse through media relations efforts.

See Reporters as Partners, not Enemies

First, leaders should acknowledge that the news media do not necessarily carry the weight that they once did. Yes, people still read, watch, and listen to the news, though increasingly in digestible bites while on a mobile device. The news cycle is 24/7, and people do not need to wait for the morning newspaper or the evening television newscast to catch up on the day's news. As well, people have more media outlets at their disposal, allowing them to consume the kind of news that appeals to their sensibility—local, national, international, liberal, moderate, conservative, and so on. All of this means news coverage is more fractured and less linear than it was prior to the Internet, and the rise of digital and social media.

Still, the news media are powerful. They exist to serve as an objective conscience, on behalf of public good. More pragmatically, news media provide third-party validation that certain issues, topics, announcements, developments, and the like are, indeed, newsworthy and of importance to the public. You can use your corporate website and social media platforms to disseminate your message, but there will never be the same type of credibility that comes with garnering the attention of, and coverage from, news media.

With that concept in mind, you should view the news media as a partner, or at least a neutral contact, rather than an enemy. You presumably are committed to moral, social, and cultural values, and journalism stands for many, if not, all of the same values and principles. Both parties want to shed light on the truth, and to bring into clearer focus the issues that are of real impact and importance to the public.

As a spokesperson, how can you communicate responsibility and build relationships with reporters, rather than brew animosity? You should strive to remain calm, clear, concise, and consistent.

Above all, stay calm. Don't let a reporter's aggressive questioning or dismissive tone set you off emotionally. Remain in control. Maintain your composure, and you maintain as much control as you will ever have with a reporter.

Likewise, remain clear in what you are saying. Don't let a reporter derail you. What helps is having two or three talking points in mind, before you talk with the reporter. Each of these points should be supported by a few facts or statistics, to help add punch and weight to what you are saying. As a reporter asks you questions, keep bringing your answers back to one of the talking points. This technique is called bridging. For example, let's say a reporter asks you during an unrelated interview whether your company would ever consider closing its local factory. You are not prepared to discuss that topic publicly, nor is that the focus of the interview. The reporter might just be digging for dirt, or trying to substantiate a rumor. In your response you might say, "Our local factory serves us well, but what we want people to know right now is . . ." and bridge to whatever that topic may be, that is, a new customer service initiative, the expansion of product distribution to a new market, etc. You are acknowledging that you have listened to the reporter's question, but you are maintaining some degree of control over the information you share.

Third, you must remain concise. The average sound bite or quotation is generally not more than 10 seconds long, or a sentence or two of text at most. That's not much. There's an absolute art to speaking concisely and clearly. This can take practice, which is something you should do with a member of your corporate communications team, or an outside agency experienced in media training (Hayes 2011).

Finally, a spokesperson should remain consistent. Your answers in today's interview should be consistent with what you share and discuss internally, and with what you share and discuss externally, with vendors, community representatives, customers, and the like. And, it should go without saying that your communication with reporters should be consistent, as well. The talking points should stay consistent, your delivery should remain consistent, and your accessibility should stay consistent, as well. Reporters like working with sources who are consistent in word, thought, and behavior. This is no different than employees who seek these same qualities in their leader. These traits are all signs of values-based leadership and responsible communication.

Research affirms that spokespersons should strive to work with reporters as partners rather than adversaries (Ulmer et al., 2007; Veil and Ojeda 2010). This is certainly true not only for crisis situations, but also for general public relations efforts. Build relationships with reporters, by reaffirming values and remaining accessible. The working dynamic will improve over time, as should media coverage.

Help Drive the News Agenda

The old adage asserts that any publicity is good publicity. Nothing could be further from the truth.

You also can't claim success by the total amount of news coverage earned. In the end, not all news media coverage is equal. At a high level, you can look at the amount of news coverage obtained, and compare that with coverage earned by your competitors. That's still too basic, though. To really understand the impact of media coverage, you have to examine tone of the mentions of your organization—positive, neutral, or negative—and whether the direct quotations and/or examples used are from your company. You also need to consider what part of the total story focused on your organization, and again compare that with any competitors mentioned.

You likely have a corporate communications team or public relations agency who can do media tracking and reporting. That shouldn't be your primary concern when it comes to analyzing, understanding, and helping drive media coverage. What matters most is getting positive coverage in the media outlets. This would be the ones that reach the right audience, and who have the greatest credibility with that audience. Given your industry, trade media might be more important than consumer media, for example. Or, if your business is more consumer-oriented, in-depth coverage in certain markets might be more important than general mentions in national media outlets. Again, you likely have a team or agency to do this analysis and strategizing. However, as a responsible communicator, you should take a vested interest in understanding your company's media relations strategy, and contributing valuable insight as appropriate.

Now, on to how to help drive the news agenda. You absolutely do not have to sit back and wait for reporters to come to you. Even the news release is becoming outdated. The coverage that matters these days is typically garnered by building relationships with key reporters over time, and pitching them story ideas and news leads, as valuable developments begin to unfold. A pitch usually takes the form of a phone call, or a brief message delivered via e-mail or private message within social media platforms like Twitter.

What stories should be pitched? Bring to mind the values your organization espouses, and think of ideas, initiatives, or successes that illustrate these values. Your communications team or counsel will usually drive this process, but they do not have to do the legwork on their own. As a leader, you often have the broadest view of the organization, and, as well, often the deepest knowledge of particular functional areas and cross-functional initiatives. You can serve your organization well by thinking of ways to build relationships with key reporters, so that the stories that affirm your organizational vision receive that important third-party validation through news media coverage.

You may be concerned about reporters and how they tend to punch holes in story ideas. Remember, this scrutinizing is their job and their social responsibility. If you anticipate concerns and think through your responses, you will be fine.

What can become challenging is national coverage of multinational operations, or local coverage of national or regional operations. The moral, social, or cultural values of a certain nation or locality might differ somewhat from the organizational values as understood in the headquarters location. In these instances, the values differences and similarities must be clearly articulated. You and your fellow leaders must have thought through these potential conflicts, and made values-based decisions with the greatest good and the least impact for all concerned. Addressing these values differences head-on can diffuse the concerns and build effective argumentation for media interviews and other purposes (Lehtimaki, Kujala, and Heikkinen 2011).

If you work in a labor-driven industry, you should pay particular attention to how the news media cover your industry and its labor practices. Media coverage pertaining to public reporting about labor standards has been found to be limited and generally favorable, across multiple different types of potential issues. Any violations receive the most extensive coverage, of course. Still, reporters provide little insight as to why certain issues exist or how those issues might be resolved (Dickson and Eckman 2008). This is where you might proactively help reporters— and, therefore, the public—understand the circumstances in which your business operates, and the values-based decisions your organization has made, or will be making.

We know that helping drive the news agenda is a viable communication strategy across many industries. In one study, for example, researchers analyzed public relations content, news media coverage, public opinion, and corporate financial performance for more than two-dozen US-based companies considered to have strong reputations. Evidence that agenda-building and agenda-setting strategies are in play, and do, in fact, help influence public opinion (Keousis, Popescu, and Mitrook 2007).

In public relations practice, most businesses focus on investors as the primary stakeholder (Moon and Hyun 2009). Businesses tend to strive, in their public relations content and news media coverage, to establish legitimacy with shareholders, rather than demonstrate some degree of power or urgency, which may come more into play with a public affairs program. People criticize business news and corporate communications for focusing too much on investors, and the evidence exists that these complaints are warranted. As a leader, you can challenge your organization to communicate more responsibly, which would be fulfilling the obligation to all stakeholders, not just investors.

Stay Accessible and Responsive

This chapter has covered considerable ground, especially if you do not currently work with the news media as a company spokesperson. The best advice may simply be to stay accessible to reporters, and responsive to their questions and concerns. Nothing good has ever been gained by ignoring a reporter, or by stating, "No comment." The public deserves better, and keep in mind that reporters are simply advocates working on behalf of the public.

Treat reporters like partners, not enemies. That means maintaining dialogue, and staying in touch. Build those relationships gradually over time, and when you really need the help of reporters who understand your organization and its values, you will be well-positioned.

Reflection Questions

- **Accessibility—Talking to a reporter can be stressful and tenuous, even when you are well prepared.** Regardless, a big part of responsible communication is owning the role of company spokesperson, and addressing the public's need for information. How confident are you, or will you be, in serving as a spokesperson? What would make you even more confident? What could you start doing now to help you better prepare for those responsibilities?

- **Responsiveness—You may be concerned about reporters and how they tend to punch holes in story ideas.** Remember, this scrutinizing is their job and their social responsibility. How might you anticipate reporters' questions and concerns? Who can help you think through appropriate responses, before you're on the spot?

- **Transparency—People criticize business news and corporate communications for focusing too much on investors.** As a leader, you can challenge your organization to communicate more responsibly, which would be fulfilling the obligation to all stakeholders, not just investors. How much of your communication agenda is driven by investors? By the news media? Should you be devoting more time to employee communications, community outreach, and other forms of responsible communication?

Responsible Actions

- **See reporters as partners, not enemies**—You presumably are committed to moral, social, and cultural values, and journalism stands for many, if not, all of the same values and principles. Both parties want to shed light on the truth, and to bring into clearer focus the issues that are of real impact and importance to the public. As a spokesperson, how can you communicate responsibility and build relationships with reporters, rather than brew animosity? You should strive to remain calm, clear, concise, and consistent.

- **Help drive the news agenda**—What matters most is getting positive coverage in the media outlets that matter the most. This would be the ones that reach the right audience, and who have the greatest credibility with that audience. As a leader, you often have the broadest view of the organization, and, as well, often the deepest knowledge of particular functional areas and cross-functional initiatives. You can serve your organization well by thinking of ways to build relationships with key reporters, so that the stories that affirm your organizational vision receive that important third-party validation through news media coverage.

- **Stay accessible and responsive**—Treat reporters like partners, not enemies. That means maintaining dialogue, and staying in touch. Build those relationships gradually over time.

CHAPTER 8

Customers and Prospects

Social media took off just prior to my transitioning to higher education. I was still doing strategy work full-time for clients, ranging from local startups and family-owned operations to Fortune 250, multinational corporations. In the span of a decade, social media went from being a novel curiosity to a nearly indispensable communication tactic, when used appropriately.

When I first started talking with clients about social media, we looked at the few platforms available as merely ways to reach young people and the tech-savvy. Most business people had little clue what social media entailed, why anyone would "waste" time using them, and what advantage there could possibly be from such an odd way to communicate. To be honest, I wasn't entirely sure, either.

If you have ever been to a trade show, you know that the challenge each year is coming up with a novel way to generate buzz and attract people to your booth. Nothing is more defeating, or costly, than investing tens of thousands of dollars on a trade show presence, only to stand around for several days, meeting few new prospects.

With a few clients, we used social media as a trade show strategy, very early on in the days of these platforms. This was long before people started thinking so intently about content strategy, and how to post the kind of information that would be both valuable and enticing to social media followers. This was also before people understood social media as a relationship-building tool, not just a way to transmit information. So, with a particular client, we would get active on Foursquare, Twitter, Facebook, and the like, but only just prior to the trade shows. We would then blast information that seemed strategic at the time, but, in hindsight, truly wasn't. By pushing out information, we thought we would attract whoever might be paying attention.

Keep in mind that this was before smart phones. So, you had people walking around a trade show, carrying their laptops in shoulder bags.

Or, worse yet, you had people getting ready for the day in their hotel rooms, or staying up late working at night, with laptops logged into the Internet, but very rarely visiting social media sites. Very few people were socially networked at that time, and even for those who were, following posts and tweets throughout the day wasn't really feasible, at least not while on the go.

We recognized these limitations, of course. And, using some old-fashioned word-of-mouth strategy, we made a point of pulling people over to our booth, and showing them what we were publishing on social media. But, you get the problem, right? We were spending a good amount of time and energy drawing people to our booth who were already near our booth, anyway. We were wasting our time telling them about our use of social media, rather than about our products and services. Even worse, we were not drawing new visitors to the booth, because so few people were social media followers at the time, and those who were did not have the convenient luxury of hand-held smart phones.

The world of social media has come a long, long, long way. In the first decade of popular usage, social media exploded. Statistics vary over time, but well more than half of online American adults participate regularly in at least one social media platform. Many are regularly active on multiple social media sites, using various platforms for different needs, both personal and professional.

You can't escape social media. As a leader, you must acknowledge that social media have simply become an extension of the real world. In fact, there isn't really a virtual world, anymore. What is happening on social media is real—that is, real dialogue, real debate, and real conversation. And all of that activity is happening in real-time, 24 hours a day, seven days per week. You cannot stop what is happening online, just as you cannot stop what is happening offline. However, with social media, you can monitor, respond, and track progress. That isn't always easy with what might be happening offline.

Whether you personally enjoy social media or not, you cannot ignore or disregard their power. You can help your organization leverage social media, through your leadership role.

Respect Digital Dialogue

What people are doing on social media matters. What they are saying about your organization, on social media, matters even more.

Consider this scenario. You own a number of small, upscale groceries serving several thriving neighborhoods in a large city. Your customers are largely affluent, highly opinionated, and active on multiple social media platforms. They might like your Facebook page, or follow your Twitter feed. That's great, but without active engagement, their likes and follows mean very little. What you want are brand advocates who engage with your team, both offline and online.

Now imagine that your upscale groceries carry free-range eggs from an area farm, and the distribution agreement is exclusive. That means the farm can sell its eggs only through your stores. When the agreement is working well, all is good. You might even pick up some positive buzz via your social media accounts. But, let's pretend that a large batch of eggs is sold that carries salmonella. Some customers escape harm, but others don't cook their eggs fully, or use them raw, and get sick. If social media did not exist, you might be able to contain the issue, take care of the customers and situation, and hope that traditional word-of-mouth doesn't spread too far or too quickly. In a world with social media, though, all of that hoping is wasted energy. People will absolutely use the technology to broadcast their concerns and complaints, just as they do their praise and admiration.

As a leader, you must respect digital dialogue. That means not placing higher value on praise received than on the criticism coming your way, especially in times of crisis. All feedback—whether positive or negative—should matter to you and your organization. With clients, I tell them to think of social media relationships as being no different than offline relationships. Social media are simply an extension of the traditional offline reality, but amped up by the speed, power, and immediacy that comes with the technology.

More than 90 percent of the Inc. 500 have been using at least one social media tool for years, and at least half of those businesses have long considered social media as very important to their business and/or marketing strategy (Barnes and Mattson 2009). These numbers continue trending up over time, meaning social media keep becoming more and more influential to growing businesses. There is an important lesson to learn from that fact. A responsible communicator acknowledges that social media have very real value—to socially-active customers, to business growth, to the end goal of staying as responsive as possible to the public's needs, wants, and concerns.

Be an advocate for social media. These platforms can be a powerful way to put organizational values into action. Just as your goal is to open up dialogue offline, so too should you want to open up dialogue offline; in fact, two-way, real-time communication is what makes social media such an important and powerful tool (Chaturvedi 2013). Help your organization be confident, diligent, and caring enough to become and stay active on social media.

Embrace Criticism; Respond Maturely

With social media activity inevitably comes highly visible, and sometimes painfully raw, public criticism. You can help your organization instill the fortitude necessary to manage through these challenges.

Solid social media management involves having clearly defined guidelines and processes for how to handle criticism. As a leader, you likely already serve as a subject matter expert for internal communications and/or news media interviews. Likewise, you should be identified and active as someone who can help diffuse social media criticism.

Guidelines would typically spell out three types of criticism to anticipate. First, there are the fairly benign remarks that can be briefly acknowledged online, then quickly and easily be moved to an offline conversation. An example might be someone whose order arrived late, and who chose to voice that complaint online rather than via a phone call or e-mail message. Your company's social media management team can quickly acknowledge the error, and direct the customer to get in contact directly for resolution, a rebate, a discount toward future purchases, or whatever.

A second category of criticisms involves highly inflammatory comments that are offensive, harassing, or blatantly false, or that make unsubstantiated allegations. Legal counsel would typically tell you never to allow such comments to fester on your social media pages, and certainly not allow yourself to be drawn into an online conversation, which could open up significant risk or liability. In these often-rare instances, the inflammatory comments are removed from the site as quickly as possible, and direct follow-up is made with the individual via a private messaging tool on that same social media platform, explaining why the comment was removed. Your responsibility as a leader is to help the social media team understand and identify the types of comments that are offensive, harassing, or blatantly false, and to defend the team's decision to police such comments when they appear.

The third category is the most troublesome. These are generally criticisms about an issue or crisis that is developing, and about which your organization is typically at fault. An example would be an airline that keeps passengers in a plane, on a tarmac, for an unreasonable amount of time. With each passing minute, more and more of these passengers, and their friends and family members, might post complaints to social media. They do this, of course, because they want—and need—to be heard. They are generally upset, and often deservedly so.

It's in these gray areas where a social media manager has to make a judgment call. Are these benign complaints, inflammatory allegations, or something in between? In the "in between" moments, this is where leaders like you can be of tremendous help. If an issue is escalating, and someone tells you that customer service call volume is spiking, you and your peers do whatever necessary to appease callers while simultaneously resolving the issue. With social media, it is no different. You may not be responsible for social media, or communication, at all. But, ultimately, your part of the organization may become part of an issue that goes public. As a responsible communicator, demonstrate leadership, and take social media criticism seriously.

The public can see what's happening on social media. I may not be a customer of your business, but perhaps my friend who lives four states away is. An issue boils up, she hops on social media, and quickly her rant gets seen by hundreds of friends and family members scattered around the nation and possibly the world. They might pass the message on, and, exponentially, the message takes hold. Inevitably, a savvy journalist will come across the posts, and investigate. Shortly thereafter, what seemed like an isolated topic becomes a full-blown crisis. And, in today's digital world, that escalation can happen in as little as a few minutes.

Become and Remain Socially Active

Of course, there is some degree of inauthenticity in becoming active on social media only when negative issues arise. A values-driven organization would view social media platforms as relationship-building tools, and acknowledge that relationships are usually healthy and enjoyable, but also occasionally troublesome and mutually frustrating. That's simply a fact of life, and in business.

Many organizations have begun to master social media as a form of responsible communication. Early pioneers included direct marketer Zappos, that has a commitment to "talk to customers every way that want to talk to us," including via social media (Clay 2012). Likewise, Marty St. George, senior vice president of marketing and commercial for upscale airline JetBlue, affirms his company's passion for social media, because the technology ". . . facilitates that one-on-one brand connection that marketers have wanted for so long" (Gianatasio 2013).

Posting to social media is, in many ways, an updated variation on old-school blogging. Does your chief executive blog, on behalf of the organization? Do you? Regardless, a blog's credibility depends on trust, and the building blocks of trust are forthrightness, openness, consistency, timeliness, truthfulness, and candor (Smudde 2005). Blogging in the traditional sense is a way of demonstrating an ongoing commitment to open, forthright communication, and shining light on what the organization values—ethically, morally, socially, and culturally.

Blogging is long-form and narrative. Micro-blogging, which is much of what happens on social media, is short-form and often actionable. You are giving people short bits that convey what you feel is important, then typically directing them to a website or infographic for more details. You might also invite opinions. All of this helps with relationship-building, but only when there is consistency, through the good times and the troubling times, as well. If your organization is not very active on social media during the good times, you are not building trust. To spike your social media activity only when bad things happen, suggests that you are defensive and largely self-oriented.

Take a cue from those who lead online discussion groups; in other words, the people perceived as the ones who foster dialogue and actively engage with others. Research shows that influencing others online comes from being active on the platform, being a credible expert, and being adaptive and responsive when it comes to posting replies and engaging in dialogue (Huffaker 2010).

Do you personally need to be on social media, representing your organization? There is a growing expectation, it seems. In fact, a recent worldwide survey revealed that more than three of every four global executives believe it is a good idea for their chief executive officer to be regularly active on social media, on behalf of the organization (Weber 2012). That does not mean, though, that being on social media for your organization is the right move. There are many considerations, not the least of which is the investment of your time, and the potential risks associated with having you communicate so visibly, and in real-time. These are matters to discuss with your communications counsel, be that an in-house communications executive or an outside consulting firm or agency.

In the end, the best role you will likely play is that of an advocate, supporting your company's social media team as needed, rather than playing the role of a direct social media personality. Be mindful that chief financial officers generally aren't as supportive of digital initiatives as chief executive officers, chief information officers, and chief marketing officers; plus, board members are generally even less supportive than the finance officers (McKinsey 2014). Digital technology, and certainly digital communication, is only going to keep exploding. The more you can advocate in this arena, the better.

Give some careful thought to how your organization uses digital communication, especially social media. How might you help infuse more of a values-driven approach? How might your expertise and ideas build more honest and meaningful relationships with stakeholders who are active on social media platforms? How can you champion digital communication with other leaders and with your team, as you strive to promote values-based decisions and initiatives?

Reflection Questions

- **Accessibility—Whether you personally enjoy social media or not, you cannot ignore or disregard their power.** You can help your organization leverage social media, through your leadership role. Are you engaged at all with your organization's social media manager or team? If so, how? If not, why not? What area of your company should have social media oversight—that is, marketing, corporate communications, customer service, information technology, etc., or some combination of these areas? Why? How can you make yourself accessible to help guide their important work?

- **Responsiveness—As a responsible communicator, demonstrate leadership, and take social media criticism seriously.** A rant seen by hundreds of friends and family members scattered around the nation and possibly the world. They might pass the message on, and, exponentially, the message takes hold. Inevitably, a savvy journalist will come across the posts, and investigate. Shortly thereafter, what seemed like an isolated topic becomes a full-blown crisis. And, in today's digital world, that escalation can happen in as little as a few minutes. How does it make you feel to see your company or its products or services criticized online? Knowing you can't control what people say about your brand on social media, how can you help address these kinds of situations? What can you do, at a higher and broader level, to try to reduce the number of instance when the public might hop on social media to complain?

- **Transparency**—More than three of every four global executives believe it is a good idea for their chief executive officer to be regularly active on social media, on behalf of the organization. Whether you are a CEO or not, are you active on social media, representing your organization? Why or why not? What signal might this send to the public?

Responsible Actions

- **Respect digital dialogue**—A responsible communicator acknowledges that social media have very real value—to socially active customers, to business growth, to the end goal of staying as responsive as possible to the public's needs, wants, and concerns. Be an advocate for social media. These platforms can be a powerful way to put organizational values into action.

- **Embrace criticism; respond maturely**—As a leader, you likely already serve as a subject matter expert for internal communications and/or news media interviews. Likewise, you should be identified and active as someone who can help diffuse social media criticism. Ultimately, your part of the organization may become part of an issue that goes public. As a responsible communicator, demonstrate leadership, take social media criticism seriously, and help respond appropriately to criticisms.
- **Become and remain socially active**—A values-driven organization would view social media platforms as relationship-building tools, and acknowledge that relationships are usually healthy and enjoyable, but sometimes troublesome and mutually frustrating. Influencing others online comes from being active on the platform, being a credible expert, and being adaptive and responsive when it comes to posting replies and engaging in dialogue.

PART 3

Leading with Values Daily— The ART Action Plan

This book had an important disclaimer upfront: it's not easy to lead an organization or operational unit and play an active role in multiple forms of communication. But, easy or not, communication is your leadership responsibility. The sooner you fully embrace this duty, the more quickly your team and your organization will benefit.

The next few pages contain a step-by-step summary of responsible actions. The first table recaps Part 1, the ART principles (i.e., accessibility, responsiveness, transparency). The remaining tables draw from each chapter of Part 2, grounded in the key principles from Part 1.

Check off the items you have already integrated, then prioritize the others. Select a new action or set of actions to incorporate each week. Soon, you will have mastered the ART of being a truly responsible communicator—committed to, actively involved in and fully responsible for robust and meaningful dialogue with all of your key stakeholders, internal and external.

Best of luck!

Key Principles: A Snapshot Refresher

Principle	Responsible Actions
Accessibility	• **Being a leader means being accessible, simple as that.** Were you not accessible to anyone, you would not be a leader. And you would not be needed.
	• **Think of each of your stakeholders, and especially each of your colleagues, as a person who requires access in order to make contributions to, and investments in, your organization's long-term success.** In the spirit of accessibility, view such situations as opportunities to engage with people who have a true passion for your business.
	• **You cannot wall yourself off in your office, delegate relationship-building to a colleague, and expect a fruitful outcome.** If the new hire or new interest needs direct access to you, then you must provide that access—not just in the short-term, but in a reliable and consistent manner over the long-term. Accessibility breeds trust, and trust builds relationships.
	• **Being accessible means staying adaptable to changing circumstances and sharing information as freely as possible, in order to help others maximize their contributions to the organization.** Being inaccessible, on the other hand, means trying to control situations and prevent access to information. Stay accessible; strive to continually put the team's needs, and not your own, first.
	• **Companies can't innovate, respond to stakeholders, or run efficiently unless people have access to timely information.** Be open, and be as candid as you can be. Seek and share information in more diverse ways. Encourage lively, respectful discussion and debate. Honor truth. Reward or at least recognize people who think differently and challenge the status quo.
	• **Be realistic.** Protect your time and energy. Prioritize your daily contacts, giving time only to those who truly need that time. Rely upon others, and delegate effectively, even when it comes to responsiveness. For every request that comes your way, think: Who should be handling this?
Responsiveness	• **Understand "responsible communication"**
	• Take accountability for clear, candid, and consistent exchange. Demonstrate daily that you care about all of the internal and external stakeholders who have a vested interest in your organization, institution, jurisdiction, or cause.
	• Listen and respond to stakeholders, and truly live your values daily. This process of voicing and fostering moral-based values requires self-discipline and self-motivation.
	• **Act with good intent**
	• Facilitate dialogue and help people feel safe speaking up and voicing their values.
	• If members of your team feel strongly about what is right in a particular situation but don't feel confident acting on their convictions, you are failing them as a leader.

	• **Foster responsiveness in others**
	  • Drive value-based communication in all aspects of your operations, with a fundamental understanding that responsible communication requires diligence and adaptability.
	  • There may not be immediate results, and the steps that helped address or resolve an issue today may not necessarily work down the road. Communication is dynamic, and, as a leader, you must remain equally dynamic.
	• **Stay accessible and responsive**
	  • You absolutely should not wait for an issue to develop, or a crisis to unfold, to get involved. As a responsible communicator, you should help identify and proactively address possible counter-arguments to your organization's performance or stance on important issues and indicators.
	  • Managing issues, and advocating for responsible communication, comes with an acceptance that few issues are ever fully resolved. You must take a long view while staying responsive and decisive in the moment.

Transparency	**Put your strengths to work**
	  • Real leadership is acknowledging that you are often the most powerful person in a room or situation. Whatever you do and say—or don't do and say—sets the tone for everyone else involved in the situation, or who may ultimately be impacted by the situation.
	  • Start from your strengths. Your communication style may not necessarily be the most effective for every situation, but stepping up and being a solid, consistent leader regardless of circumstances is crucial
	• **Advocate honesty 24/7**
	  • Simply managing to the numbers, and rewarding or penalizing based on performance, will not significantly improve employee buy-in and spur organizational growth.
	  • What is more likely to drive morale and positive change is honesty about economic challenges and organizational circumstances, and responsiveness to employees' concerns and suggestions.

Stakeholder Group: Managers and Supervisors

Principle	Responsible Actions

Accessibility	• **Model desired behavior**
	  • Help others understand how and why you make certain decisions, and the values which inform those important choices.
	  • Communicate effectively in multiple ways; become adept at adapting your approach with stakeholders, as necessary.
	  • Take an active interest in communication plans, and/or how communication challenges are addressed as part of larger strategic plans.

Responsiveness	• **Commit to shared principles**
	  • As a leader, you sign on to be involved in tough decisions, and to understand that your role is to move the organization, not your personal agenda, forward.
	  • What you do and how you act, particularly on issues and initiatives that are not yet employee or public knowledge, is pivotal.

Transparency	• **Hold peers accountable**
	  • Organizations must evolve over time, and change is exceptionally difficult for individuals. Be the leader that people need.
	  • Effective change is more likely when people believe a change initiative is needed, has been designed appropriately, that organizational capability exists, that leaders believe in the change, and that the change will ultimately benefit them personally in some way.

Stakeholder Group: Employees and Contractors

Principle	Responsible Actions

Accessibility	• **Foster a dynamic culture**
	  • You should be doing something, or perhaps even many things, every day to help shape the kind of culture your organization needs to survive and thrive long-term.
	  • A cultural champion tries to make the work environment as dynamic as possible for everyone involved. This means actively engaging with people, to understand what they need and want in order to do their jobs better, and to feel more satisfied and valued at work.
	  • This is rarely a one-size-fits-all conversation, though. Make accommodations to tailor communication to individuals and their unique differences and preferences.

Responsiveness	• **Listen and respond in person**
	• By sparking conversation, you put others at ease, and help them feel more willing to raise their own voices. You demonstrate that you value hearing thoughts and opinions, and that, regardless of the situation, there is always time and space for conversation.
	• Of course, confidential, private, personal, and/or sensitive information is best handled face-to-face and one-on-one. While face-to-face communication is not always feasible, one-on-one communication usually is. A discreet phone call, when necessary, can be as personal and meaningful as a face-to-face conversation, especially when time and/or distance don't allow for a personal meeting.
	• Use your best judgment, but always, always try to personalize your approach when the message is of a sensitive nature.
Transparency	• **Drive true organizational change**
	• The more you can do now to foster a dynamic, supportive climate should help dramatically when the time comes for organizational change, or when a crisis inevitably occurs. Continuous efforts by leaders to improve communication and ease employees' apprehension have been shown to result in more positive employee behaviors and less negative employee feedback during times of corporate crisis.
	• A culture with leaders who model and encourage positive behavior can influence how employees interpret traditionally "bad news" messages. Employees in this kind of culture are resilient and optimistic when "bad news" hits, and they tend to focus on organizational strengths, rather than whatever threat is at hand.
	• As always, your responsibility is to foster responsible communication. That means keep values first and foremost in your mind, and the minds of those from whom you are trying to garner support. That means talking honestly about the values that are driving this decision, and how this large-scale organizational change will help bolster organizational values for the long-term. That also means making sure each step in the communication and change process involves dialogue, and not simply dictating of orders.

Stakeholder Group: Investors and Regulators

Principle	Responsible Actions

Accessibility	• **Keep pace with the market**
	  • Whatever your functional area, you should be paying attention to industry trends and particularly analysts' and policymakers' opinions.
	  • When it comes to the market, be aware that investors tend to react most enthusiastically to news items regarding new customers, completion of acquisitions, strategic long-term decisions, and nontechnological alliances.
	  • You should be creating and encouraging mutually helpful discussions with investors and policymakers about values-based issues and decisions.

Responsiveness	• **Answer the tough questions**
	  • Analysts and policymakers are increasingly asking tough questions, as they should. Think about how you might help answer those tough questions. Your subject matter expertise could prove particularly valuable.
	  • Have you thought of offering to sit in on an analyst call or be part of a lobbying effort? Remember, you have important stories to share, but you also could benefit from valuable feedback, criticism, and dialogue.

Transparency	• **Look ahead, mitigate risk**
	  • Anticipate counter-arguments to the stories and successes you wish to share inside your organization and with the public.
	  • Your personal values, or those of your corporation, may not necessarily be values shared or respected by your stakeholders, including investors, analysts, and policymakers.
	  • Every decision you make or help champion comes with trade-offs and downsides. Be honest about these concessions; their human, financial, and environmental impacts; and the perceptions they may generate from those who not involved in the decision-making process.

Stakeholder Group: Editors and Reporters

Principle	Responsible Actions

Accessibility	• **Help drive the news agenda**
	  • What matters most is getting positive coverage in the media outlets that matter the most. This would be the ones that reach the right audience, and who have the greatest credibility with that audience.
	  • As a leader, you often have the broadest view of the organization, and, as well, often the deepest knowledge of particular functional areas and cross-functional initiatives. You can serve your organization well by thinking of ways to build relationships with key reporters, so that the stories that affirm your organizational vision receive that important third-party validation through news media coverage.

Responsiveness	• Stay accessible and responsive • Treat reporters like partners, not enemies. That means maintaining dialogue, and staying in touch. Build those relationships gradually over time.
Transparency	• See reporters as partners, not enemies • You presumably are committed to moral, social and cultural values, and journalism stands for many, if not, all of the same values and principles. Both parties want to shed light on the truth, and to bring into clearer focus the issues that are of real impact and importance to the public. • As a spokesperson, how can you communicate responsibility and build relationships with reporters, rather than brew animosity? You should strive to remain calm, clear, concise, and consistent.

Stakeholder Group: Customers and Prospects

Principle	Responsible Actions
Accessibility	• Respect digital dialogue • A responsible communicator acknowledges that social media have very real value—to socially active customers, to business growth, to the end goal of staying as responsive as possible to the public's needs, wants and concerns. • Be an advocate for social media. These platforms can be a powerful way to put organizational values into action.
Responsiveness	• Embrace criticism; respond maturely • As a leader, you likely already serve as a subject matter expert for internal communications and/or news media interviews. Likewise, you should be identified and active as someone who can help diffuse social media criticism. • Ultimately, your part of the organization may become part of an issue that goes public. As a responsible communicator, demonstrate leadership, take social media criticism seriously, and help respond appropriately to criticisms.
Transparency	• Become and remain socially active • A values-driven organization would view social media platforms as relationship-building tools. Acknowledge that relationships are usually healthy and enjoyable, but sometimes troublesome and mutually frustrating. • Influencing others online comes from being active on the platform, being a credible expert, and being adaptive and responsive when it comes to posting replies and engaging in dialogue.

Acknowledgments

Oddly enough, a historical research fellowship with the Arthur W. Page Center for Integrity in Public Communication is what sparked the idea for this forward-thinking book. Page is often considered the founder of corporate public relations in the United States. Researching Page's career got me thinking about the importance of how leaders communicate today, both the leaders who manage public relations activities and especially those who do not.

My gratitude to Business Expert Press, especially Mary Gentile, Rob Zwettler, and the rest of the team. They have been incredibly supportive.

I must also thank the many executives, clients, contractors, colleagues, and students with whom I have worked over the years. You have listened, sometimes begrudgingly, when I insist that responsible communication is not simply a support function, a service-for-hire, or a one-way push. Indeed, responsible communication is candid, clear, and consistent—and always, always, always a dynamic, two-way process. My expertise as a consultant and coach would not exist without the diverse experiences we have shared.

Several experts reviewed working drafts of the manuscript. Special gratitude goes to author and retired executive, Carol Bodensteiner, who has long been a mentor and friend. She brought particularly valuable insight to my work.

Finally, this book honors my father, Donald, who, like Page, worked in telecommunication, and my mother, Valeria. They taught me so much about effective communication and personal responsibility.

Bibliography

Introduction

Gentile, M. *Giving Voice to Values: How to Speak Your Mind When You Know What's Right*. Ann Arbor, MI: Sheridan Books, 2010.

Krauss, C. "Leadership Trends: Busy CEOs Spend Most of the Week Managing Communications and in Meetings." *Yahoo! Finance / BusinessWire*. May 6, 2014.

Silverman, S. E. "Where's the Boss? Trapped in a Meeting." *Wall Street Journal*. February 14, 2012.

Part 1

Chapter 1

American Bar Association. *Model Code of Professional Responsibility*. (1969). http://www.americanbar.org/groups/professional_responsibility/publications/model_rules_of_professional_conduct.html

Arbab K. B., Spaulding, A., Johnson, C. E., and Gamm, L. "Success Factors for Strategic Change Initiatives: A Qualitative Study of Healthcare Administrators' Perspectives," *Journal of Healthcare Management* 59, no. 1 (2014): 65–81.

Gentile, M. *Giving Voice to Values: How to Speak Your Mind When You Know What's Right*. Ann Arbor, MI: Sheridan Books, 2010.

Gottlieb, J., and Willmott, P. *The Digital Tipping Point: McKinsey Global Survey Results*. (2014). http://www.mckinsey.com/insights/business_technology/the_digital_tipping_point_mckinsey_global_survey_results

Hazley, G. "Frustrated Journo Groups Tell Obama PA Officers Stymie Reporting." *O'Dwyer's: Inside News of Public Relations and Marketing Communications*. July 9, 2014.

Herring, K. "Management in Real Life: Top Communicators." *Management Quarterly* 49, no. 4 (2008): 28–31.

Hyatt, M. Leadership, Success and Accessibility. *Michael Hyatt: Helping Leaders Leverage Influence*. June 26, 2012. http://michaelhyatt.com/leadership-success-accessibility.html

Ketchum. *Leadership Communication Monitor*. (2014). http://www.ketchum.com/leadership-communication-monitor-2014

Koffler, K. Obama Abolishes the Press Conference. *White House Dossier*. May 4, 2012. http://www.whitehousedossier.com

Northouse, P. G. *Leadership: Theory and Practice*. Thousand Oaks, CA: SAGE Publications, 2010.

O'Toole, J., and Bennis, W. "What's Needed Next: A Culture of Candor." *Harvard Business Review* 87, no. 6 (2009): 54–61.

Potter, P .B. K, and Baum, M. A. "Looking for Audience Costs in All the Wrong Places: Electoral Institutions, Media Access, and Democratic Constraint." *Journal of Politics* 76, no. 1 (2014): 167–81.

Quast, L. *New Managers: 4 Reasons You Need an 'Open Door' Policy*. October 7, 2013. http://www.forbes.com

United Nations General. Assembly.*Convention on the Rights of Persons with Disabilities*. 2006. http://www.un.org/disabilities/convention/conventionfull .shtml

Vielmetter, G., and Sell, Y. "Leadership Is About to Get More Uncomfortable." *Harvard Business Review Blog Network*. July 1, 2014. http://blogs.hbr.org

Waligo, V. M., Clarke, J., and Hawkins, R. "The 'Leadership-Stakeholder Involvement Capacity' Nexus in Stakeholder Management." *Journal of Business Research*, 67, no. 7 (2014): 1342–52.

Chapter 2

Bowen, S. "A State of Neglect: Public Relations as 'Corporate Conscience' or Ethics Counsel." *Journal of Public Relations Research* 20, no. 3 (2008): 271–296.

Dresp-Langley, B. "The Communication Contract and Its Ten Ground Clauses." *Journal of Business Ethics* 87, no. 3 (2009): 415–36.

Forman, J. "Leaders as Storytellers: Finding Waldo." *Business Communication Quarterly* 70, no. 3 (2007): 369–73.

Gentile, M. *Giving Voice to Values: How to Speak Your Mind When You Know What's Right*. Ann Arbor, MI: Sheridan Books, 2010.

Grossman, D. *You Can't Not Communicate*. Bloomington, IN: AuthorHouse, 2010.

Hyatt, M. *Are You a Responsive Person?* July 27, 2011. http://www.michaelhyatt .com

Marken, G. A. "Corporate Communications: It's All About Delivering Value." *Public Relations Quarterly* 6, no. 2 (2001): 39–40.

Martin, J. H., and Grbac, B. "Using Supply Chain Management to Leverage a Firm's Market Orientation." *Industrial Marketing Management* 32, no. 1 (2003): 25–38.

Meyer, C., and Kirby, J. The Big Idea: Leadership in the Age of Transparency. *Harvard Business Review* 88, no. 4 (2010): 38–46.

Murphy, P. "Developing, Communicating and Promoting Corporate Ethics Statements: A Longitudinal Analysis." *Journal of Business Ethics* 62, no. 2 (2005): 183–9.

Oliveira, M F. "The Leader as the Face of a Crisis: Philip Morris' CEO's Speeches During the 1990s." *Journal of Public Relations Research* 21, no. 4 (2009): 361–80.

Robles, M. M. "Executive Perceptions of the Top 10 Soft Skills Needed in Today's Workplace." *Business Communication Quarterly* 75, no. 4 (2012), 453–65.

von Groddeck, V. "Rethinking the Role of Value Communication in Business Corporations From a Sociological Perspective: Why Organizations Need Value-Based Semantics to Cope with Societal and Organizational Fuzziness." *Journal of Business Ethics* 100, no. 1 (2011): 69–84.

Werder, K. P., and Holtzhausen, D. "Organizational Structures and Their Relationships with Communication Management Practices: A Public Relations Perspective from the United States." *International Journal of Strategic Communication* 5, no. 2 (2011): 118–42.

Chapter 3

Arvidsson, S. "Communication of Corporate Social Responsibility: A Study of the View of Management Teams in Large Companies." *Journal of Business Ethics* 96, no. 3 (2010): 339–54.

Bernard, J *Business at the Speed of Now: Fire Up Your People, Thrill Your Customers, and Crush Your Competitors.* Hoboken, NJ: Wiley, 2011.

Bock, H. *The Case for Transparency in Leadership.* April 3, 2012. http://www.clomedia.com

Carr, A. "Punk, Meet Rock: Inside Airbnb's Grand Hotel Plans," *Fast Company,* April 2014, 75–112.

Dando, N., and Swift, T. "Transparency and Assurance: Minding the Credibility Gap." *Journal of Business Ethics* 44, no. 2–3 (2003): 195–200.

DeKay, S H. "Doing What's Right: Communicating Business Ethics." *Business Communication Quarterly* 74, no. 3 (2011): 287–88.

Gentile, M. *Giving Voice to Values: How to Speak Your Mind When You Know What's Right.* Ann Arbor, MI: Sheridan Books, 2010.

Halter, M. V., and de Arruda, M. C. C. "Inverting the Pyramid of Values? Trends in Less-Developed Countries." *Journal of Business Ethics* 90, no. 3 (2009): 267–75.

Jadhi, K., and Acikdilli, G. (2009). "Marketing Communications and Corporate Social Responsibility (CSR): Marriage of Convenience or Shotgun Wedding?" *Journal of Business Ethics* 88, no. 1 (2009): 103–13.

Jaques, T. "Issue Management as a Post-Crisis Discipline: Identifying and Responding to Issue Impacts Beyond the Crisis." *Journal of Public Affairs* 9, no. 1 (2009): 35–44.

Llopis, G. *5 Powerful Things Happen When a Leader Is Transparent.* September 10, 2012. http://www.forbes.com

Massey, J. E. "Managing Organizational Legitimacy: Communication Strategies for Organizations in Crisis." *Journal of Business Communication* 38, no. 2 (2001): 153–82.

Meyer, C., and Kirby, J. The Big Idea: Leadership in the Age of Transparency. *Harvard Business Review* 88, no. 4 (2010): 38–46.

Michener, G., and Bersch, K. "Conceptualizing the Quality of Transparency." Paper presented at the Global Conference on Transparency, Rutgers University, Newark, NJ, 2011.

Pies, I., Beckmann, M., and Hielscher, S. "Value Creation, Management Competencies, and Global Corporate Citizenship: An Ordonomic Approach to Business Ethics in the Age of Globalization." *Journal of Business Ethics* 94, no. 2 (2010): 265–78.

Pontefract, D. "Rethinking the Work of Leadership." *Harvard Business Review Blog Network.* July 12, 2013.

http://blogs.hbr.org

Rawlins, B. "Give the Emperor a Mirror: Toward Developing a Stakeholder Measurement of Organizational Transparency." *Journal of Public Relations Research* 21, no. 1 (2009): 71–99.

Tilley, E. "The Ethics Pyramid: Making Ethics Unavoidable in the Public Relations Process." *Journal of Mass Media Ethics* 20, no. 4 (2005): 305–20.

Wagner, T., Lutz, R. J., and Weitz, B. A. "Corporate Hypocrisy: Overcoming the Threat of Inconsistent Corporate Social Responsibility Perceptions." *Journal of Marketing* 73, no. 6 (2009): 77–91.

Part 2

Chapter 4

De Vries, R. E., Bakker-Pieper, A., and Oostenveld, W. (2010). "Leadership—Communication? The Relations of Leaders' Communication Styles with Leadership Styles, Knowledge Sharing and Leadership Outcomes." *Journal of Business Psychology* 25, no. 3 (2010): 367–80.

Gentile, M. *Giving Voice to Values: How to Speak Your Mind When You Know What's Right.* Ann Arbor, MI: Sheridan Books, 2010.

Kotter, J. "Leading Change: Why Transformation Efforts Fail." *Harvard Business Review* 73, no. 2 (2005): 59–67

Meng, J., Berger, B., Gower, K. K., and Heyman, W. "A Test of Excellent Leadership in Public Relations: Key Qualities, Valuable Sources, and Distinctive Leadership Perceptions." *Journal of Public Relations Research* 24, no. 1 (2012): 18–36.

Murphy, P. "Developing, Communicating and Promoting Corporate Ethics Statements: A Longitudinal Analysis." *Journal of Business Ethics* 62, no. 2 (2005): 183–9.

Simoes, C., Dibbs, S., and Fisk, R. "Managing Corporate Identity: An International Perspective." *Journal of the Academy of Marketing Science* 33, no. 2 (2005): 153–68.

Torppa, C., and Smith, K. L. (2011). "Organizational Change Management: A Test of the Effectiveness of a Communication Plan." *Communication Research Reports* 28, no. 1 (2011): 62–7.

Chapter 5

David, G. "Internal Communication: Essential Component of Crisis Communication." *Journal of Media Research* 10, no. 2 (2011): 72–81.

French, S. L., and Holden, T. Q. "Positive Organizational Behavior: A Buffer for Bad News." *Business Communication Quarterly* 75, no. 2 (2012): 208–20.

Gentile, M. *Giving Voice to Values: How to Speak Your Mind When You Know What's Right.* Ann Arbor, MI: Sheridan Books, 2010.

Kupritz, V., and Cowell, E. "Productive Management Communication: Online and Face-to-face." *Journal of Business Communication* 48, no. 1 (2011): 54–82.

Madlock, P., Martin, M. M., Bogdan, L., and Ervin, M. "The Impact of Communication Traits on Leader-member Exchange." *Human Communication* 10, no. 4 (2007): 451–64.

Mayfield, J., and Mayfield, J. "The Role of Leader-motivating Language in Employee Absenteeism." *Journal of Business Communication* 46, no. 4 (2009): 455–79.

Mazzei, A., Kim, J., and Dell'Oro, C. "Strategic Value of Employee Relationships and Communicative Actions: Overcoming Corporate Crisis with Quality Internal Communication." *International Journal of Strategic Communication* 6, no. 1 (2012): 31–44.

Mueller, B. H., and Lee, J. "Leader-member Exchange and Organizational Communication Satisfaction in Multiple Contexts." *Journal of Business Communication* 39, no. 2 (2002): 220–44.

Northouse, P. G. *Leadership: Theory and Practice.* Thousand Oaks, CA: SAGE Publications, 2010.

Schullery, N. (2013). "Workplace Engagement and Generational Differences in Values." *Business Communication Quarterly* 76, no. 2 (2013): 252–65.

Smith, J. M. "All Good works are Not Created Equal: Employee Sensemaking of Corporate Philanthropy." *Southern Communication Journal* 77 no. 5 (2012): 369–88.

Tucker, E. *Five Best Practices for Fostering a Culture of Communication.* Human Capital Institute. July 24, 2013. http://www.hci.org

Chapter 6

Cuellar-Fernandez, B., Fuertes-Callen, Y., and Lainez-Gadca, J. A. "The Impact of Corporate Media News on Market Valuation." *Journal of Media Economics* 23, no. 2 (2010): 90–110.

Hockerts, K., and Moir, L. "Communicating Corporate Responsibility to Investors: The Changing Role of the Investor Relations Function." *Journal of Business Ethics* 52, no. 1 (2004): 85–98.

Kelley, K. S., Laskin, A. V., and Rosenstein, G. A. "Investor Relations: Two-way Symmetrical Practice." *Journal of Public Relations Research* 22, no. 2 (2010): 182–208.

Murrey, D. W. *Perspectives on Best Practices in Dealing and Communicating with the Investment Community.* (2013). http://www.rrdonnelley.com

Northouse, P. G. *Leadership: Theory and Practice.* Thousand Oaks, CA: SAGE Publications, 2010.

Penning, T. "The Value of Public Relations in Investor Relations: Individual Investors' Preferred Information Types, Qualities, and Sources." *Journalism & Mass Communication Quarterly* 88, no. 3 (2011): 615–31.

Pettigrew, J. E., and Reber, B. H. "The New Dynamic in corporate Media Relations: How Fortune 500 Companies are Using Virtual Press Rooms to Engage the Press." *Journal of Public Relations Research* 22, no. 4 (2010): 404–28.

Chapter 7

Dickson, M. A., and Eckman, M. "Media Portrayal of Voluntary Public Reporting about Corporate Social Responsibility Performance: Does Coverage Encourage or Discourage Ethical Management?" *Journal of Business Ethics* 83, no. 4 (2008): 725–43.

Hayes, G. "Beyond Memorization: A Guide to Coaching Executives for the Media." In *PR News' Media Training Guidebook.* Edited by Goldstein S., 124–6. Rockville, MD: PR News Press, 2011

Keosuis, S., Popescu, C., and Mitrook, M. "Understanding Influence on Corporate Reputation: An Examination of Public Relations Efforts, Media Coverage, Public Opinion, and Financial Performance from an Agenda-building and Agenda-setting Perspective." *Journal of Public Relations Research* 19, no. 2 (2007): 147–65.

Lehtimaki, H., Kujala, J., and Heikkinen, A. "Corporate Responsibility in Communication: Empirical Analysis of Press Releases in a Conflict." *Business Communication Quarterly* 74, no. 4 (2011): 432–49.

Moon, S. J., and Hyun, K. D. "The Salience of Stakeholders and their Attributes in Public Relations and Business News." *Journal of Mass Media Ethics* 24, no. 1 (2009): 59–75.

Ulmer, R R., Seeger, M. W., and Sellnow, T. "Post-crisis Communication and Renewal: Expanding the Parameters of Post-crisis Discourse." *Public Relations Review*, 33, no. 2 (2007): 130-134.

Veil, S. R., and Ojeda, F. "Establishing Media Partnerships in Crisis Response." *Communication Studies* 61, no. 4 (2010): 412–29.

Chapter 8

Barnes, N. G., and Mattson, E. "Social Media in the 2009 Inc. 500: New Tools and New Trends." *Journal of New Communications Research* 4, no. 2 (2009): 70–9.

Chaturvedi, M. *Effective Social Media Strategies–Four Tips, Four Benefits.* (2013). http://www.oracle.com/us/corporate/profit/big-ideas/042213-mchaturvedi-1937903.html

Clay, K. *Why Business Should Use Social Media for Customer Service.* November 30, 2012. http://www.forbes.com

Gianatasio, D. *JetBlue Knows How to Communicate with Customers in Social, and When to Shut up.* September 9, 2013. http://www.adweek.com

Huffaker, D. "Dimensions of Leadership and Social Influence in Online Communities." *Human Communication Research* 36, no. X (2010): 593–617.

McKinsey. *McKinsey Global Survey: The Digital Tipping Point.* (2014). http://www.mckinsey.com/insights/business_technology/the_digital_tipping_point_mckinsey_global_survey_results

Smudde, P. "Blogging, Ethics and Public Relations: A Proactive and Dialogic Approach." *Public Relations Quarterly* 10, no. 3 (2005): 34–8.

Stephens, K. K., and Malone, P. C. "If the Organizations Won't Give us Information. The Use of Multiple New Media for Crisis Technical Translation and Dialogue." *Journal of Public Relations Research* 21, no. 2: 229–39.

Vorvoreanu, M. "Perceptions of Corporations on Facebook: An Analysis of Facebook Social Norms." *Journal of New Communications Research* 4, no. 1 (2009): 67–86

Weber S. *The Social CEO: Executives Tell All.* (2012). http://www.webershandwick.com/uploads/news/files/Social-CEO-Study.pdf

About the Author

In the first few decades of his career, David Remund designed and managed corporate-wide strategic communications programs for Bank of America, Principal Financial Group, and multiple divisions of Wells Fargo & Company. He has served as an agency director of strategic planning, as well, and continues to consult and coach independently, in addition to teaching full-time at the University of Oregon.

Remund's research focuses on how professionals develop leadership and communication competencies, learn to adapt and collaborate effectively, and maintain their personal values despite competing demands. He has published in multiple venues, including *Journal of Consumer Affairs, Journal of Leadership Studies, Public Relations Review, Teaching Journalism and Mass Communication, Teaching Public Relations,* and *PR News' Guidebook to Media Relations.*

Remund is a past fellow of the Plank Center for Leadership in Public Relations, and the Arthur W. Page Center for Integrity in Public Relations. He earned his doctorate from the University of North Carolina at Chapel Hill, and has been nationally accredited by the Public Relations Society of America since 2003.

Index

Accessibility, 3–11
    definition of, 4–5
    of editors, 68–69
    handling of, 8–9
    reasons for, 5–8
    reflection questions, 10
    of reporters, 68–69
    responsible actions, 11
    and transparency, link between,
        31–32
    trust and, 6
American Bar Association, xii

Bernard, John
    Business at the Speed of Now, 27
Blogging, 76
Bridging, 65

Chesky, Brian, 31
Communication, 14–15, 22
    e-mail, 47–48
    face-to-face, 47
    one-on-one, 47
    responsible, 15–16, 21
Contractors, 45–56
    dynamic culture, fostering, 49–53
    listening and responding in person,
        46–49
    organizational change, driving,
        53–54
    responsible actions, 84–85
Convention on the Rights of Persons
        with Disabilities, 4
Criticism, handling, 74–75
Cultural champion, 50
Customers, 71–79
    becoming active on social media,
        75–77
    criticism, handling, 74–75
    digital dialogue, respecting, 72–74
    reflection questions, 77–78
    responsible actions, 78–79, 87

Digital dialogue, respecting, 72–74
Dynamic culture, fostering, 49–53

Editors, 63–70
    accessibility of, 68–69
    news agenda, driving, 66–68
    reflection questions, 69
    responsible actions, 69–70, 86–87
    responsiveness of, 68–69
E-mail, 47–48
Employees, 45–56
    dynamic culture, fostering, 49–53
    listening and responding in person,
        46–49
    organizational change, driving, 53–54
    reflection questions, 55
    responsible actions, 55–56, 84–85

Face-to-face communication, 47

Gentile, M., 52
    Giving Voice to Values, xiii, 6–7,
        39, 47

Integrity, 22
Intent, act with, 18–21
Investors, 57–62
    pace with market, keeping, 58–59
    reflection questions, 61
    responsible actions, 62, 86
    risk-mitigation, 60–61
    tough questions, answering, 59–60

Ketchum, 5
Kotter, J., 41

Leader-member exchange theory
        (LMX), 7, 50–51
Leadership peers, holding, 41–42
LMX. See Leader-member exchange
        theory (LMX)

Managers, 37–43
    commit to shared principles, 39
    leadership peers, holding, 41–42
    model desired behavior, 40
    reflection questions, 42
    responsible actions, 42–43, 84
Micro-blogging, 76
Model desired behavior, 40

National Investor Relations
        Institute, 59
News agenda, driving, 66–68

Obama's communication legacy, 8–9
One-on-one communication, 47
Organizational change, 53–54

Pace with market, keeping, 58–59
Partners, reporters as, 64–66
Philip Morris, 19–20
Pontefract, D.
    Flat Army: Creating a Connected and
        Engaged Organization, 38
Productive leader, 8
Prospects, 71–79
    becoming active on social media,
        75–77
    criticism, handling, 74–75
    digital dialogue, respecting, 72–74
    reflection questions, 77–78
    responsible actions, 78–79, 87
Public Relations Society of America, 59

Regulators, 57–62
    pace with market, keeping, 58–59
    reflection questions, 61
    responsible actions, 62, 86
    risk-mitigation, 60–61
    tough questions, answering, 59–60
Reporters, 63–70
    accessibility of, 68–69
    news agenda, driving, 66–68
    as partners, 64–66
    reflection questions, 69
    responsible actions, 69–70, 86–87
    responsiveness of, 68–69

Responsible communication, 21
    definition of, 15–16, 24
Responsiveness, 13–24
    act with intent, 18–21
    definition of, 16
    of editors, 68–69
    importance of, 16–18
    in others, fostering, 21–23
    reflection questions, 23–24
    of reporters, 68–69
    responsible actions, 24
    and transparency, link between,
        31–32
Responsibility, definition of, xii
Risk-mitigation, 60–61

Sell, Yvonne, 9
Shared principles, commit to, 39
Social media, becoming active on,
        75–77
St. George, Marty, 76
Strengths to work, and transparency,
        29–30
Supervisors, 37–43
    commit to shared principles, 39
    leadership peers, holding, 41–42
    model desired behavior, 40
    reflection questions, 42
    responsible actions, 42–43, 84

Total transparency, 27
Tough questions, answering, 59–60
Transparency, 25–34
    and accessibility, link between, 31–32
    definition of, 26–27
    honesty, advocating, 30–31
    importance of, 27–29
    reflection questions, 33
    responsible actions, 33–34
    and responsiveness, link between,
        31–32
    strengths to work and, 29–30
    total, 27
Trust, and accessibility, 6

Vielmetter, Georg, 9

THE GIVING VOICE TO VALUES ON BUSINESS ETHICS AND CORPORATE SOCIALRESPONSIBILITY COLLECTION

Mary Gentile, Editor

The Giving Voice To Values initiative teamed up with Business Expert Press to produce a collection of books on Business Ethics and Corporate Social Responsibility that will bring a practical, solutions-oriented, skill-building approach to the salient questions of values-driven leadership. Giving Voice To Values (GVV: www.GivingVoiceToValues.org)—the curriculum, the pedagogy and the research upon which it is based—was designed to transform the foundational assumptions upon which the teaching of business ethics is based, and importantly, to equip future business leaders to not only know what is right, but how to make it happen.

There are over a dozen more titles coming out in this collection, later this year and through 2015.

Announcing the Business Expert Press Digital Library

Concise e-books business students need for classroom and research

This book can also be purchased in an e-book collection by your library as

- a one-time purchase,
- that is owned forever,
- allows for simultaneous readers,
- has no restrictions on printing, and
- can be downloaded as PDFs from within the library community.

Our digital library collections are a great solution to beat the rising cost of textbooks. e-books can be loaded into their course management systems or onto student's e-book readers.
The **Business Expert Press** digital libraries are very affordable, with no obligation to buy in future years. For more information, please visit **www.businessexpertpress.com/librarians.** To set up a trial in the United States, please contact **Adam Chesler** at adam.chesler@businessexpertpress.com. For all other regions, contact **Nicole Lee** at nicole.lee@igroupnet.com.

www.ingramcontent.com/pod-product-compliance
Lightning Source LLC
Chambersburg PA
CBHW071209200326

41519CB00018B/5441

9 781606 497548